Around the Lakeland Hills

By The Same Author

Lore of the Lake Country

Around the Lakeland Hills

F. J. CARRUTHERS

ROBERT HALE · LONDON

First published in Great Britain 1976

ISBN 0 7091 5690 1

Robert Hale Limited
Clerekenwell House
Clerkenwell Green
London EC1R 0HT

Filmset by Specialised Offset Services Limited, Liverpool
and printed in Great Britain by
Lowe & Brydone Limited
Thetford, Norfolk

Contents

Illustrations

Acknowledgements

The author's thanks are due to Sir John Burgess and Cumberland Newspapers Ltd, for permission to use material which was written in other forms for various newspapers of the Group; to Mr B.G. Jones, the County Archivist and his staff at Carlisle Castle, and the librarians and staffs at Tullie House, Carlisle; Whitehaven, Workington and Cockermouth public libraries for many kindnesses; Mr Daniel Hay, of Whitehaven, who is a mine of information on many subjects; and Mrs J.B. Wivell, who supplied information on 'coaching days' from records kept by her grandfather.

To
MADELINE

Introduction

Quiet, lifeless and rather sad museum piece encased, as some would have it, in a cover of restrictions, or live, vigorous, activated by the young in heart and the young in body?

That seems to be the choice in any controversy raging about the Lake District today. There was no such choice yesterday, in all those yesterdays which make up a couple of centuries of 'laking', because the area was alive with a hard-working and hard-playing indigenous population and a rising tide of visitors and off-come residents who, by and large, made the Lake District what it is today. That some of their buildings and activities were far more outrageous than would be countenanced today is beyond question; it is also beyond question that neither they nor their activities ruined the district of the Lakes, a fact from which those who are today anxious about the area's future should draw some comfort.

The Lake District is now, perhaps, more attractive than it has ever been. And accessible with it. 'Crowded', they call Lakeland today, and there are murmurs of protest about 'over-advertisement' which the environmentalists and many modern 'lakers' consider unnecessary, even dangerous, since the motorways brought the National Park within easy reach of some of the most heavily populated parts of the country. Perhaps it is crowded by the standards of that quite recent yesterday when Ulpha Moor was a lonely place in high summer, when a single party could have all of Pillar Rock to themselves, and when the only time and place with a queue for a climb was Whit or August Monday at Napes Needle.

But still, by any standards the Lake District is, over most of its area, a vast emptiness. The crowds flock to the towns and their gift shops, and only the enthusiasts – and school parties – head for the hills. However, crowds in the towns included, and allowing for the decline of dales farming, there are still more sheep than people, and when Keswick's Main Street and the pierhead at Bowness are suffering invasions comparable with the crowds on Blackpool's 'Golden Mile', it is possible in a few minutes to be far enough from the madding crowds for one's presence upon its heaf to make a Herdwick hogg stamp its feet in anger at the intrusion on *its* peace and quiet.

Earlier generations who discovered the Lakes indulged themselves far more outrageously than the ice cream-licking, gum-chewing visitors of today, and left quite indelible marks upon its fair face, and on its history too. The feet of today's visitors wear the soil off Friar's Crag and beat a pathway up Helvellyn, but nobody can build a mansion just to enjoy a view, and there would be considerable opposition to any proposal to build a bonfire of tar barrels on Skiddaw.

More than eyebrows would be raised today if there was to be a replay of Squire Pocklington's celebrated mock battle on Derwentwater, or if somebody were to put a cannon-armed boat on Ullswater just to "test the echo".[1] The A66 is an emotive subject today, but neither the road it replaces along Bassenthwaite Lake shore nor the railway whose course it follows existed when the Lakes stage coaches were at the height of their popularity. So once upon a time *that* road was new, and, as it happened, was welcomed when it was built.

There cannot be anybody who had more regard for the Lakes than Robert Southey and William Wordsworth, yet those two pre-eminent 'lakers' could be found, in 1815, engaged in rather undignified cavortings on Skiddaw's summit to celebrate the victory at Waterloo, a 'do' which would have had the modern amenities societies raising protests.

This book is mainly about people in the Lakes: natives and off-comers who won for themselves and for the countryside in which they had chosen to live different sorts of notice which vary from the sublime to the ridiculous.

One thing which is outstanding about the Lake Country in

its past is that whatever the attitude or behaviour of the visiting off-comer, the natives have always shown a tolerance which is, by the standards of many modern 'lakers', beyond all understanding; or which has been accounted for by a particularly vociferous, disappointed holidaymaker as follows: "Of course they are tolerant! They have to be. If they can put up with the Cumbrian weather, they can tolerate anything!"

That exclamation could be interpreted as a slander. Among other things, this book explains that Lake Country weather is not as bad as it seems from a set of dull figures or the oft-repeated 'claim' that it has "the wettest place in Europe".

A supreme example of tolerance was that of Dr David Lietch, a Scoto-English off-come with a gift for careful observation and colourful description, who gave up his dream of a retirement cottage at the foot of Skiddaw because it was the whim of a materialistic Wordsworth that he should do so.

Tolerant too were the native Lakelanders of Percy Bysshe Shelley when that young, newly-wed and runaway, idealistic but disinherited and near-bankrupt poet brought his illusions into the district. Shelley – or maybe his landlord Gideon Dare – was the exception which proved the rule because the poet came under pressure to leave, and nobody was sorry when he went.

If the Cumbrians had to be tolerant about the weather and the visitors and resident off-comers, they had also to be tolerant of a somewhat monotonous diet born of the necessity of a way of life based on the subsistence farming of the valleys. But they did live long and healthy lives, and though porridge, or 'poddish', may not be the elixir of life Canon Rawnsley made it out to be, the humble oat did for many generations of Cumbrians what rice has done for far more generations of Asians.

Men seeking freedom from the shackles of modern living have found that freedom in the Lakes. There are some who could, for want of a better word, be called 'hermits', although some were merely tramps who stopped tramping. But almost all of these people, who might today be called 'drop-outs', were tolerated, even welcomed, and found, some of them, a sort of Heaven on an earth which had not been over-generous.

There is a chapter about coaching in the Lake District, a traffic development which brought the first flush of 'lakers'; about the men who drove the coaches and guarded the mail; and about one of them who almost deprived the country of its Poet Laureate.

The mention of fox-hunting today tends to heighten passion in many people, but the Lake Country brand of fox-hunting requires no defence as long as lambs are worried and poultry stolen on dales farms by foxes which show no signs either of remorse or of becoming extinct, although the fell footpacks account for up to 400 'Reynards and Reynardines' in a season.

The story is told of Mally Messenger because Dr Lietch called her to memory in some of the best pages in his *Notebook* which the *West Cumberland Times* published in instalments before the start of this century, and the story is also told of Askew Peel's horse-deal with 'Pigtail' Armstrong in vindication of that other, more famous Peel, John, because at least two of John Peel's biographers have put this somewhat dubious, perhaps childish transaction on the famous hunter's record.

It comes as a surprise to most people to learn that a great initiative in solving the mystery of that king of fish, the Atlantic salmon, was taken in a remote, hidden valley of the Lake District, Troutdale, where the remains of the fish-rearing tanks still mystify that lovely little valley's infrequent visitors.

That there must be another, seamier side of life in the Lake District is inevitable now as it was in days long ago, and the 'Ouse Bridge Incident' is worth recording from reliable sources because the truth of such incidents tends to be lost in a tangled web of folklore which evolved in years of telling the tale at home firesides or to wagonette-loads of people *en route* from West Cumberland to Castle Inn.

In a lifetime spent in the hills and around there have been many 'days to remember', and what could be more memorable than being among the climbing party which, as a fiftieth birthday treat for a truly great Lady of the Lakes, accompanied her on an ascent of what is perhaps the finest rock climb in the Lake District – Scawfell's Central Buttress.

1

No Warning for Shepherds

The Cumbrians' preoccupation with weather is understandable. They are not allowed to forget that within the bounds of the county is "the wettest place in Europe". This gem of local knowledge does not surprise the holidaymaker who arrives when the weather is in its most tetchy mood; the devout 'laker' doesn't care.

"The wettest place in Europe" tag has been given to Seathwaite in Borrowdale, which is unfortunate for Seathwaite because it is not the wettest place. The title really belongs, according to the early records, to somewhere above Sty Head top in the neighbourhood of Sprinkling Tarn,[1] but the wrongful labelling is understandable because in the days when such titles were bestowed, a 'place' had to be where somebody lived: a village, a recognizable location, and Sprinkling Tarn was not, in the terms of a century or so ago, a recognizable location. In Cumbria we would call it a 'spot' rather than a 'place'.

That notwithstanding, Seathwaite remains indelibly marked as the wettest place, although this writer has never, in innumerable visits, been there on a wet day.

That, to anybody acquainted with Lake District weather, is quite understandable.

Weather is unpredictable in any part of the Lakes. The "red sky in the morning, shepherd's warning" has little relevance in a district where the only portent of rain is the sight of a grey curtain of it advancing up or across a valley, and when sunshine can only be predicted when the sun is seen about to emerge from behind the cloud.

Who can predict weather where it is possible to stand dry on one side of a road and watch people getting wet on the other side? What is the point of trying to predict when one valley's rain can be blown in minutes into the next valley? It is one of few places where it is possible to get some morbid enjoyment out of watching a rainstorm happening to somebody else.

Possibly the only reliable weather portent in this area is the 'bar' and the yellowing of the sky which heralds the coming of the 'helm' wind, probably because Nature concedes that frail humans must be given notice of such a violent occurrence: a wind that can lift rocks out of screes, stacks out of fields, and was, according to some local lore, the original "wind that blew the turnips up".

The 'helm' occurs mostly on the western side of Cross Fell, but it has its counterpart at Honister where it is called "The wind in the Crack". In 1848 'the Crack' lifted John Rigg, a quarryman, off Long Man and threw him down Honister Crag to his death.[2]

Any weather lore that exists in the Lakes seems to accept the rain as inevitable, and none attempts to predict the weather of a following day, which is an exercise at which even the experts of the Meteorological Office have little success.

In Keswick they used to quote:

> Morlan fluid[3]
> Ne'er did good.

This was a plain statement of the fact that if it rained on the day Keswick held its Morlan (or Magdalen, or Leather) Fair on the day of St Mary Magdalen, it would ruin the fun to be got out of this festival.

Years of experience of the climate of his native county led one of the greatest scientists of the time, John Dalton, propounder of the Atomic Theory, to predict the weather on strictly non-scientific lines for it is recorded that once at Buttermere he abandoned a project to visit Pillar in Ennerdale because, in his own words, "there was not as much blue sky as would make a pair of breeches".[4]

But if the people of the Lakes did not have any reliable, or quotable, weather portents for the immediate future, they did sometimes try long-range forecasting, and the old *Shepherd's Calendar* of 1626 suggested that the key month for weather signs was January and the crucial dates the 12th and the 14th. It said: "If on January 12th the sun shine, it foreshadows much wind. If on January 14th, St. Hilary, the sun shine brightly, we shall have more wind than water", which was about as accurate a weather prediciton as the one we still hear about St Swithin's Day, or that other about the oak and the ash and the soak and the splash.

Many people certainly are disgruntled about the Lake District weather, particularly day-trippers in their Sunday best trying to make the best of things when the mountain tops are condensing water out of the clouds at a prodigious rate. True lovers of the Lakes come prepared, mentally and physically, so that they do not seem to mind whether it rains or not. The physical preparation is important, but the rain has a penetrative quality which defies the most elaborate and expensive of rainwear and wets the wearer nevertheless. Most hardened fell-walkers choose garments which will 'turn' rain and allow the body to breathe, albeit eventually allowing the rain to penetrate, rather than those which are as waterproof as the skin of a kayak, on the premise that the perfect waterproof is also a perfect sweat trap and wets its owner from the inside.

Waterproofs, as such, have never been totally accepted in the Lakes. Local people take a wetting as a natural hazard of residence, and many make only a token attempt at protection, like that immortalized by the equally immortal Mrs Heelis, famed farmer and Herdwick sheep-breeder of Sawrey, who, according to her local contemporaries who believed in putting first things first, also "wrote books about a rabbit".

Mrs Heelis, who was of course Beatrix Potter, when going about her farming business, wore for protection against the rain a sack with one corner turned in to form a sort of helmet for her head, the rest of the sack covering her shoulders. It is a sort of 'raincoat' still very much in favour among fell farmers, but hessian sacks are difficult to come by today, and the modern plastic sack is "nut t' seame".[5]

In order to enjoy the Lakes it is essential to be either waterproof, or able to take a joke and recover from a wetting, because there's nothing that will stop rain coming down.

When it was raining past the bounds of normal endurance in southern Lakeland they used to say, "We'll hev ta git a Langden lid", which was an echo of a time when an old man of Little Langdale was asked by a visitor, "How can you live in such rain?" The dalesman replied, "Whey, it's bad eneuf, but we're thinking o' hevin' a lid put on."

Most of the people seen today walking the roads, footpaths and fells, and, inexplicably in the eyes of the stranger, not looking very miserable about it, have accepted the advice given to a visitor by a Keswick ancient who said that if it rained they "mun deu as they deu under Skiddaw." When the visitor was foolish enough to ask what they did at Underskiddaw when it rained, the old Keswickian replied, "They let it."

One of the few weather sayings which survive is:

> If Skiddaw hath a cap,
> Scruffel wots full well of that.

This bears out the suggestion that Cumbrian weather lore is comment and not forecast because the implication here is that bad weather spreads. This saying in itself underlines the uncertainty felt even in concocting this little comment because it has never been decided whether the 'Scruffel' which wots full well of Skiddaw's cap is Scawfell or Galloway's Criffel.

One of the better-known items of weather lore owes its origin to nothing worse than a despondent 'laker'. It was entered in the visitors' book at a Lakeland hotel during a protracted spell of bad weather:

> Thirty days hath September,
> April, June and November.
> From January until May
> The rain it raineth every day.

All the rest have thirty-one
Without a blessed beam of sun,
And if any of them had two and thirty
They'd be just as wet and twice as dirty.

But there is, surely, no weather forecast so gloomy as that, again from the *Borrowdale Almanac* and published in the *Derwentwater Record* of 8 September 1856. The *Almanac*, claimed to be "never failing", is almost a cry for help:

When the wind's in the south it is certain to rain,
When in the north rain descendeth again;
When there's no wind at all the rain will come down,
And if in the east, with a lowering frown,
The clouds seem to say "There'll be rain very soon".
When west you may have a gleam of sunshine or two,
Though great are the odds that you don't get wet through.

Well, nobody has ever advertised 'Sunny' Lakeland, so nobody can be accused of gilding the lily for the tourist or the longer-stay visitor, and no matter what the weather brings, the district is usually full and overflowing – with people as well as water.

Nevertheless the Lake District does have long, warm, dry spells, otherwise Derwentwater's famous floating island[6] would never float, and there are several people, visitors and residents, who will treasure for the rest of their lives the sight they saw at Grange-in-Borrowdale's two-humped bridge in the spring of 1974.

A film crew had arrived in Borrowdale to make a film in which a steady downpour of rain was a 'must'. And there they were making their film with rain being pumped out of the Derwent and sprayed on the actors by a fire engine borrowed from the Workington station! It hadn't rained in Borrowdale for weeks; hiring the fire engine was an act of sheer desperation on the part of the producer. For the rest of 1974 it rained quite regularly.

Somebody had to make the momentous discovery that within the bounds of Cumbria there was a spot which could claim the title of "the wettest place in Europe". The honour fell to a Cumbrian: a Whitehaven man, John Fletcher Miller.

He was not a pioneer in the study of meteorology. One of the pioneers was that other Cumbrian, John Dalton, who was born in the hamlet of Eaglesfield, near Cockermouth. Dalton brought the inquisitiveness and vision of the scientist to the study of natural phenomena and, in the words of Henry Lonsdale in *Worthies of Cumberland*, "raised the science of meteorology from its speculative and fanciful surroundings" – in other words the web of myth and mystery which had been woven around weather in a mass of old rhymes and proverbs – "to the sober region of inductive methods".

It was Lonsdale who commented that it had possibly benefited Dalton in his studies that he spent the first twenty-six years of his life in Cumberland "where Jupiter Pluviosis too often reigns as an unmerciful deity". Dalton, however, was not interested in measuring rainfall. As befitted one of the greatest scientists of the day, he was expected to lead a life devoted to experiment, but, unlike the showmen among the scientists who sought to impress by making flashes and bangs, Dalton went about it more quietly, devoting his time to such things as analysing air samples for oxygen and nitrogen content, experiments which he was able to carry out among the Cumberland hills. In January 1826 he reported that air taken from the summit of Helvellyn was "considerably inferior in oxygen to the air below" – which was the dawn of the realization which was eventually to lead mountaineers into taking cylinders of oxygen with them up Everest and similar high places.

Dalton's method of sampling the air at the summit of Helvellyn was simple. He got somebody – usually it was his old friend Jonathan Otley, the Keswick clock-maker, geologist and writer of guide-books – to carry a large bottle of water to the summit where the water was emptied out and, presto! – a bottle of Helvellyn summit air.

The prevalence of a rainfall in the Lake District comparable with that found in Southern India only became known after Dalton had died, and John Fletcher Miller brought that devastating fact to public notice. Miller, like Dalton, came from a Quaker family and was educated at the school in Kendal which John Dalton and his brother had built up in reputation. He wanted to be a doctor, but was in delicate health himself and so he turned instead to literature and the natural sciences.

He was only fifteen when he started his local meteorological register recording the weight and temperature of the air, rainfall and wind direction and force. He moved on to measure surface evaporation, radiation of heat from the earth's surface, and conduct other experiments. He wrote essays for the *Philosophical Transactions* of London, and *The Edinburgh Philosophical Journal* which aroused some interest, sufficient to encourage him to explore new fields.

In 1844 he started his series of experiments on the fall of rain in the Lake District which he conducted with data collected from as many as thirty rain gauges which he set up in various parts, one of them right on the summit of Scawfell.

Miller commented: "Some remarkable results were elicited", which was an understatement because his essay, read to he Royal Society by Colonel Sabine on 18 May 1848, created a sensation.

The sensation arose from the revelation that there was, here in England, a place where the average annual rainfall was nearly 150 inches. The place was Sprinkling Tarn, then called Sparkling Tarn, 1900 feet above sea level.

In his essay Miller stated: ". . . it will be perceived that the downfall of rain at Seathwaite and its adjacent stations exceeds the annual receipts at most of the stations in the peninsula of India . . ."

He found that in general the heaviest rainfall was at the eastern extremities of the dales, the moist, warm, west winds being subject to the effects of the mountains which in fact acted liked giant condensers.

At Sprinkling Tarn, Miller reported, the rainfall occasionally amounted to 180 inches annually, and the rainfall of a single month had in very wet seasons exceeded 30 inches, as was the case at Seathwaite, Gatesgarth and Langdale Head in December 1852.

The maximum daily rainfall he recorded was nearly 7 inches.

It was of some interest then, as it still is, to discover that the maximum rainfall was achieved at a height of approximately 2000 feet above sea level, and that the driest parts of the Lake District are the summits of some of the fells. Miller had found out, in his great wanderings among the fells, that it was possible to stand on top of a mountain in bright sunshine while the mist-shrouded valleys below were in the throes of rainstorms. His rain-gauge readings confirmed that this was evidence of a weather tendency rather than an occasional incident.

Equally amazing were his findings about the temperatures of different parts of the district. At a time when the distant valleys of the Lakes were regarded as being less than hospitable in hard winters, he discovered that the temperatures at the valley heads were several degrees higher than the temperatures at lower altitudes and on the gentler landscapes of the Cumberland plains. This, he concluded, was because the condensation of rain from moisture-saturated clouds generated sufficient heat to raise the temperatures of the valleys.

He reported: "The amount of heat yielded up annually in the formation of 141 inches of rain at Seathwaite is almost incredible, and the extent to which the climate of this naturally inhospitable region is ameliorated by this natural provision of equalising temperature must be proportionately great."

Miller's findings on the "wonderful" (the adjective is Lonsdale's) rainfall among the Cumberland fells were not believed by some of the scientists of the day, even after they had received the commendation of the Royal Society by its publication of them, but there has been more than enough confirmation since Miller's death in 1856, principal support coming from his cousin J.W. Fletcher, who, apart from being M.P. for Cockermouth, was a man with a similar scientific bent. Some of Fletcher's figures made Miller's seem conservative, notably those of the year 1866 when Fletcher recorded a rainfall of 224.56 inches at Sty Head.

Miller's records were kept on reams of quarto paper filled with columns of figures and thousands of words in impeccable copperplate writing and in themselves seemed a useful life's work, but he was not altogether the single-minded, dedicated scientist.

He had time also for observing Nature in her gentler moods, and while he kept to a strict schedule in making his scientific observations, he left it to the natural sequence of events to hail the arrival or speed the passing of a season.

Spring for him was not a period on the calendar, but a time of birds nesting, leaves sprouting and primroses blooming.

On 14 April 1853, he found Nature's own signs of spring more encouraging than any other portents, and recorded: "It is a fine sunny day and I found a blackbird's nest containing four, and a thrush's nest containing three eggs, the latter near Bridgefoot . . . The hedgerows are only beginning to bud and the only green leaves visible are the wild gooseberry and the woodbine. On warm banks primroses are expanding in considerable number."

Miller regularly covered the vast distances a circuit of his gauge stations required, once covering a total of 70 miles in a single expedition. His self-imposed task might have been easier if he had chosen to work from a base more central to the sites of his gauges, but he preferred to work from the observatory he had built at Whitehaven, a small circular building with a conical copper roof set in a lofty position above the new road.

Throughout western Lakeland his tall, athletic figure was well known. Sometimes he walked alone, sometimes, if he could find one who could match his pace, with a friend. It was difficult to believe that this was a man once considered too weak for the rigours of a doctor's life. He strode along the roads and up the western valleys of the Lake District with the long loping stride of the fellman, commenting all the time on the wonders and beauties of Nature around him. Every expedition was a voyage of discovery for him, an absorbingly interesting lecture for anybody in his company.

In his observatory he became absorbed in his writing, tabulating invaluable and interminable data. When 1853 came in like the proverbial lion of March with a gale which lasted four days, he noted the gale, but was too busy to notice the aftermath. He recorded: "At four o'clock the atmosphere assumed an orange tinge which had a very peculiar effect upon surrounding objects, resembling the lurid atmosphere of the landscape during a solar eclipse", an entry which might have gone down as his own observation had it not been for the honesty of the scientist which made him admit: "I was busy writing at the time, but I was told about it by a scientific gent . . ."

That must indeed have been a startling month for the general public as well as for the scientific observer because Miller also noted a fall of black rain. "Some parts of High Furness", he wrote, "were so black as to darken the mountain brooks and even the earth over which they flowed."

This black rain which was probably a result of air pollution in those early days of the Industrial Revolution in the area, was regarded as a portent of a change in the weather, and Miller duly noted what it portended, and the change which actually came a few days later, for on 19 January West Cumberland had its first bright clear night since the previous November.

The settled weather continued until April arrived; a fortnight later he found his nests and spring had arrived.

April proved a fruitful month for the observer of natural phenomena and Miller recorded both solar and lunar haloes, and on the 27th a brilliant shooting star.

May Day brought the first taste of summer, but winter had its final fling on the 9th and covered the fields between Cockermouth and Keswick with snow.

June, reported Miller, was gorgeous, and summer continued along a fairly normal Lakeland pattern until the cutting of fields of grain heralded the approach of winter.

Gales and thunderstorms ushered in winter; there were sharp frosts in December, and on Christmas Day, to show that even scientists had time to occupy with other matters, he merely noted: "Rain."

That was the last full year for which Miller kept up observations. Feeling now that he had given meteorology all he had to give, he told family and friends in 1855 that he now intended to enter himself at Guy's Hospital and return to his boyhood dream of becoming a doctor. But his health began to fail, and he died in July 1856. He is buried in the cemetery of St James's church, Whitehaven.

Great though the contribution was that John Fletcher Miller made to our knowledge of the Lake District weather and its principal causes and effects, it is unlikely that he will ever be regarded as the favourite historical character of any of the Lake District amenities societies. If somebody had discovered vast deposits of gold in the mountains, they could not have posed a more serious threat of despoilation than Miller's discovery, and revelation to the country at large, that here in England was a place which had a heavy annual rainfall spread quite evenly through the year . . . a rainfall as high, in aggregate, as that of tropical India.

To English cities where the cry of the day was for sanitary reform, with piped supplies of pure water as the first priority, his discoveries were like the manna that fell for the Israelites in the morning. Already in 1875, Lonsdale was eagerly anticipating the inauguration of schemes for extracting water from this "home of rain" for Newcastle and Gateshead who were reported to be interested; for Liverpool, and even for London.

At that time, Manchester was not even among the runners.

2

Skiddaw Under Fire

"Such night in England ne'er had been
Nor e'er again shall be ...

Macaulay, 'The Armada'

Unless heroic peoms are no longer fashionable in school curricula, Macauley's 'The Armada' is well known to everybody. It sends the blood of the patriot racing with "rugged miners" pouring to war "from Mendip's sunless caves" as the rousing rhymes of the poet rush the warning fire over all England by way of St Michael's Mount and Beachy Head, and Longleat's towers and Cranbourne's oaks until

This time of slumber was as bright and busy as the day.

On and on the warning beacons, calling all England to arms, sped up the country until the fire reached Lancaster Castle, and

Skiddaw saw the fire that burned on Gaunt's embattled pile,
And the red glare on Skiddaw roused the burghers of Carlisle.

A fine climactic end to a poem which has aroused the blood of generations of Englishmen, reduced to bathos by the late Tom Wilson, of Keswick, historian and doer of numerous good things for 'his' town, who once wryly remarked that "the burghers still take some rousing", which is a fairly average West Cumbrian comment on the people of the county capital and particularly on those who administer the county's business.

Macauley's poem, however, was just the sort of thing to arouse pride in one's country and its history, to build up morale; to induce a sense of occasion.

Canon H.D. Rawnsley,[1] Vicar of Crosthwaite, a co-founder of the Naitonal Trust; author and poet, and honorary chaplain to King Edward VII, was a patriot if ever there was one. The sixth sense with which he was well endowed was a sense of occasion which caused him to produce a reminiscence of and a poem for almost every occasion which arose. Such an occasion was the tercentenary of the defeat of the Spanish Armada which fell due in July 1888.

What better, said the Canon, than that history should be repeated and that a beacon should burn on Skiddaw's summit.

He had had his appetite for bonfires whetted a year earlier when Queen Victoria's Golden Jubilee had been celebrated with a bonfire on Skiddaw, but Rawnsley felt that the tercentenary of the defeat of the Armada should be an occasion when the fires would burn all over England, and if the rest of England did not respond, or even care, then they at Keswick certainly would, and the whole world would know about it.

Canon Rawnsley was an excellent organizer. He had a way with him. He was the sort who said "We shall do this or that", and then the local populace ran around obeying orders. Not that the Keswick folk minded; they too liked a good bonfire.

So the menfolk and the boys spent weeks collecting and carrying material for the fire up Skiddaw, a considerable haul, as anybody will agree who has made the long trek up to the summit from the Keswick side. That was still a time when most visitors thought it almost the limit of human endurance to get to the top unaided, unladen and on foot. It was still a time when ponies were hired to carry visitors up the mountain, and when the famous old 'Half-way House'[2] was regarded as an important staging post on the ascent, providing an opportunity for rest and refreshment, as well as being a kind of Skiddaw 'Rubicon' for it was here that the final decisions were made whether to press on for the summit or descend, defeated, back into town.

Rising to the occasion, the businessmen and the gentlefolk of Keswick and district contributed liberally to the cost of bonfire material which included forty cartloads of peat, several tar barrels and a great quantity of old timber and brushwood.

It was, as the *West Cumberland Times* said, "no light undertaking to raise a pyre of such dimension at so high an altitude". Most of the material was carted up, a tremendous task for both men and horses, but some was carried in individual back-loads by men and boys.

As a starter for the bonfire, to ensure that it got well under way in the shortest time possible, Canon Rawnsley commanded that the pyre would require to be soaked in the fastest-burning fuel then known: petroleum, and his willing helpers hauled more than eighty gallons of that highly inflammable fluid to Skiddaw top in glass Winchesters and demi-johns.

On the evening of the anniversary, 19 July, a good proportion of the population of Keswick walked up Skiddaw to watch the operation from close range, the rest remaining below to watch. Of course, Rawnsley himself went up the mountain, and with him went Mrs Rawnsley who was to light the bonfire. Among those present was M.J.B. Baddely, author of the famous 'Guides' who happened to be in Keswick on business at the time.

A long crocodile of people wended their happy way up the mountainside. There was refreshment, for those requiring it, at the Half-way House – at prices which caused some of the customers to jib, but the custodian of the Half-way House continued to charge somewhat higher-than-usual prices for his wares into modern time because he had to ensure that he was repaid for his trouble in hauling lemonade, ginger beer and dandelion and burdock stout to the little hut. Scaling what the old writers called "the mighty monarch of the Lakes" was always a thirst-inducing business.

At the top the bonfire was an imposing pile nearly 30 feet high, and it took Messrs Hall and Howell, the official bonfire builders and minders, a full hour to pour all the available oil and petroleum over this great mass of straw, bracken, timber and peat.

While Hall and Howell were going about their business, the Canon, never loath to give a lecture on almost any subject under the sun, gathered some of the crowd around him and, standing on a barrel, gave a graphic account of the defeat and destruction of the Spanish Armada. The Canon's sense of occasion dictated that if there was a celebration going on, people should never be in any doubt about what was being celebrated, and from contemporary accounts it appears that he did tend to treat the more lowly of his parishioners – and some of the higher-placed ones as well – as being educationally backward.

At ten o'clock precisely two rockets were fired as a signal that the 'do' was about to commence, and Mrs Rawnsley, carrying a long pole to which a burning torch had been fixed, stepped forward to light the fire.

It almost became the last step she ever took. It had been a happy thought on somebody's part to fasten the torch to a long pole and not take the good lady to within striking distance of the immense flash of flame which shot outward as well as upward as the petrol caught fire. Mrs Rawnsley leapt back to safety and a great cheer went up from the crowd.

Joy was unconfined. More rockets were fired, one or two creating minor incidents before it was realized that bottles which had recently been full of petrol were not the best or safest launching pads of rockets.

Edward Highton, the local schoolmaster, and ever a faithful Rawnsley disciple, had been under orders to recite Macauley's poem from end to end, and this he did, standing on the barrel the Canon had used as a platform when he delivered his lecture. Manfully, Highton recited the poem, although hardly a word could be heard over the din of exploding rockets, the crackling of burning timber, and the general jollifications which had developed around the fire.

Then somebody in the crowd decided that it would be a good idea to 'chair' the organizer, so Rawnsley was seized and hoisted shoulder-high and marched round the bonfire, the crowd singing 'Rule Britannia'.

Pocket flasks and sandwich cases appeared and the top of

Skiddaw in the light of that great anniversary bonfire and in the warmth of a July night became a giant picnic area.

More patriotic songs were sung, more rockets were fired, and then, an hour after the bonfire had been lit, the crowd began slowly to wend their way down the path from Skiddaw summit, everybody agreeing that it had indeed been a grand night.

A slight damper was put on the event because, long as they looked, they could not see another bonfire on any of the other Lakeland peaks – or anywhere else – which aroused some doubt as to the veracity of Macauley's account, already under question because there was some doubt whether a fire which burned "on Gaunt's embattled pile" could be seen from anywhere further north than Coniston Old Man. It didn't help much when it was discovered that many of the good people of Keswick hadn't seen it either. However, it was agreed that the town had had a good advertisement from the bonfire. Something had to be said which would make the exercise seem worthwhile. Carlisle, it is reported, was completely unmoved by the "red glare on Skiddaw".

As Tom Wilson said: the burghers "took a bit of rousing".

There had been other Skiddaw bonfires, apart from the one which celebrated Queen Victoria's Golden Jubilee. One was on the night of Monday 21 August 1815, when, albeit two months late, Robert Southey and friends marked another famous victory, Waterloo.

"Never", wrote Southey to his brother, who was a doctor at the Middlesex Hospital,

> was such an assemblage upon such a spot . . . Lord Sunderlin rode up, and Lady S., who had endeavoured to dissuade *me* from going up as a thing too dangerous, joined the walking party. Wordsworth with his wife, sister, and eldest boy, came over [from Rydal] on purpose. James Boswell [son of Dr Johnson's companion] arrived that morning at the Sunderlins'. Edith, the Senhora,[3] Edith May and Herbert were my convoy, with our three maid-servants; some of our neighbours, some adventurous lakers, and Messrs Rag, Tag and Bobtail made up the rest of the assembly. We roasted beef and boiled plum puddings there, sung 'God save the King' round the most furious body of flaming tar

barrels that I ever saw; drank a huge wooden bowl of punch; fired cannon at every health with three times three, and rolled large blazing balls of tow and turpentine down the steep side of the mountain. We formed a huge circle round the most intense light, and behind us was an immeasurable arch of the most intense darkness, for our bonfire fairly put out the moon.[4]

In his letter, Southey mentioned a "mishap which . . . will make a famous anecdote in the life of a great poet, if James Boswell, after the example of his father, keepeth a diary of the sayings of remarkable men."

The 'mishap' was the knocking over of the kettle, with the water boiling in it, which had been intended for the punch. At such a time and in such a place this was a calamity, water being, as Southey pointed out, "a commodity not easily replaced on the summit of Skiddaw". So an investigation was set afoot to discover the culprit.

From people standing by at the time it was learned that the kettle had been knocked over by a "gentleman wearing a red cloak", which instantly identified the culprit as Wordsworth who was wearing a cloak he had borrowed from Edith Southey. His punishment was that all his friends gathered round him and sang "'Twas *you* that kicked the kettle down! 'Twas you, Sir, you!" What gem of repartee this drew from the future Poet Laureate was not recorded either by Southey or Boswell.

The immediate problem on Skiddaw top was to replace the water, and this was done by 'Appropriating' water from other people, and while the ladies and gentlemen had their punch, their myrmidons and Messrs Rag, Tag and Bobtail had to drink their rum neat, which had the effect of livening up proceedings which were already lively enough.

Care was thrown to the wind. "All our torches were lit at once by this mad company, and our way down the hill was marked by a track of fire," wrote Southey, and Sarah Coleridge, in a letter to Thomas Poole, described the long line of bobbing, descending torches as "a most uncommon and beautiful effect".

Mrs Coleridge had remained in Greta Lodge to view proceedings from there in the company of Sir George

Beaumont[5] who had intended to join in the jollifications at the summit, but had been imprudent enough to climb Skiddaw that forenoon and dare not attempt a second ascent.

Both Sarah Coleridge and Southey said that the bonfire was in celebration of "our great victories", but, Macauley not yet having written 'The Armada', they were unconcerned whether or not the red glare on Skiddaw had caught the attention of the burghers of Carlisle.

News travelled quite slowly in the early years of the nineteenth century, but news of the defeat of Napoleon at Waterloo was in England within twenty-four hours. Some time later it got through from the capital to the corners of the land, but the initial enthusiasm for the victory seemed to have faded somewhat by the time the Lake poets and their friends decided to celebrate the victory. Waterloo was fought and won on 18 June 1815, so the *Cumberland Pacquet* could be excused for being slightly befogged as to the reason for the bonfire in August. Although Robert Southey and Co. were explicit that the bonfire was in celebration of Waterloo, the *Pacquet* assumed that because of the date chosen for it (originally 12 August) it was to celebrate the birthday of the Prince Regent. That it was also the birthday of the Duke of Wellington seemed, to the *Pacquet*, to be a mere incidental.

However, the *Pacquet*'s account of the preamble to the bonfire is interesting because it says that the weather on the 12th was so bad that the lighting of the bonfire had to be postponed "till a better opportunity offered". The *Pacquet* adds some information which Southey had apparently not considered worth recording. After mentioning the postponement, the newspaper says: "We are sorry the story does not end there. A set of miscreants assembled in the night, ascended the very summit of the mountain, and early next morning [Sunday] dispersed and burned all the articles consisting of tar barrels, oil casks, peat, ling & c which had been collected for the purpose." Which proves that vandalism is not a purely twentieth-century phenomenon, and that Canon Rawnsley was correct in insisting that *his* bonfires should be guarded at night.

However, Keswick's loyalty, seldom, if ever, in question, was burning fiercely, and the *Pacquet* went on to announce that "notwithstanding this defeat of a very local effusion by a brutal act of malevolence (we are credibly informed) the towering head of Skiddaw will still shine with increased splendour the first clear evening."

And shine it did, as Southey says. And of this great "illumination of Skiddaw" on 21 August, the *Pacquet* said:

> A great concourse of people ascended the mountain upon which several pieces of beef were roasted and plum pudding boiled, of which all present ate – at least tasted through curiosity. The health of the Prince Regent, the Duke of Wellington and Prince Blucher were drunk with three times three over an immense bowl of punch royal, each of the toasts being announced to the world below by the dischage of a cannon, and 'God Save the King' and 'Rule Britannia' were sung in full chorus accompanied by a band of music.

The *Pacquet* listed the important people who had been among the assembly on Skiddaw summit, and added that the festivities concluded with fireworks at Keswick.

The real celebration of the Waterloo victory seems, in the eyes of *Pacquet* reporters, to have been the great fireworks display on 26 August at Derwent Bank where Lord Sunderlin had taken up temporary residence. Derwent Bank was

> most brilliantly illuminated . . . in commemoration of the Battle of Waterloo . . . In front of the house were three transparencies, the first representing the great bonfire on Skiddaw by an eminent female artist, the second John Bull, on a cask with a can of ale in his hand revealing Buonoparte with the devil on his shoulders, the devil in the act of dropping Buonoparte into the lake – not into Derwent Lake, but in the lake which is described as abounding, not with trout, perch and pike, but with fire and brimstone. This is said to have been designed by one of the foremost artists in the kingdom. A grand display of rockets, wheels, Roman candlesticks etc., with some aquatic fireworks were exhibited to several hundred people collected from all the neighbouring places to view the festive scene which closed with the ascent of a fire balloon ten feet high and eighteen feet in circumference.

On this occasion, seventy-three years back from Rawnsley's famous "red glare on Skiddaw", the bonfire was reported by the *Carlisle Journal* as having been "discerned at fifty miles distance", from which it is assumed that this time the burghers of Carlisle, or some of them, had seen it.

Typically, perhaps understandably in view of the dilatoriness of the celebrants, the burghers got the wrong message, and the *Carlisle Journal* omitted any mention of Waterloo, stating plainly that the bonfire was "in honour of the Prince Regent's birthday".

3

Coaching Days

"The coachmen adorned in their white topper hats,
Some wearing smart leggings, some buttoned spats;
A'tooting their horns, and a'cracking their whips,
And making the most of their everyday trips."

Ballads of a Coach Driver,
by John W. Lewthwaite

There is no doubt that the old coaches had what we today call 'style'. That is probably a reason why driving four-in-hand is back in fashion for those who can afford it. Even the men who drove the coaches had style, and though they sprang from humble families, they could make their fortunes, and in so doing achieve reputations which have become part of the history of the districts they and their coaches served.

The drivers had the enviable job, and there was hardly a lad who did not dream of driving a four-in-hand with the dash of a mail coach driver, as generations of boys a century later dreamt of spending long hours with hands on the throttle of the Royal Scot or the Flying Scotsman.

The coach guards had the responsibility and a more resplendent uniform because they had to wear the official red as servants of the Crown when it was the Royal Mail they were guarding.

We seem to regard the coach as having been with us since the beginning of civilization: the natural successor to that earlier conveyance-cum-battle wagon, the chariot, and that it has been in use continuously since the Romans convinced our ancient forefather Britons that their practice of fitting scythe blades to the hub-caps was dangerous to pedestrians under the *Pax Romana.*

In fact the passenger coach came in only after centuries of disuse had made the admirable road system which the Romans had built in their most northerly province utterly unusable by wheeled traffic.

Queen Elizabeth I was one of the pioneers of coaching in this country. Nobody less than a queen could have the authority to turn out entire local populations to ensure a passably smooth route for the royal conveyance. Packhorses could do their carrying perfectly well across common land or on the quagmires they called roads, and as long as England's economy remained based on the self-sufficiency of communities, there was little need for better communications.

The early coaches were no better than carts because springing had not been invented, and there is a record of the Virgin Queen complaining bitterly at an audience she gave the French ambassador of her boneshaking experience in a coach driven too fast a few days previously.

Gradually the coaching habit caught on and eventually the stage coach came along and catapulted England into an age of cheap and relatively fast transport.

By 1672 there were only six regular coaches running throughout the kingdom, but six were, in the opinion of John Crisset of the Charterhouse, far too many. He wrote a pamphlet urging the suppression of the coaches on the grounds that they were undermining the social structure of Britain as it then existed.

"These stages", he wrote,

> make gentlemen come to London on every small occasion, which otherwise they would not do but upon urgent necessity, nay the convenience of the passage makes their wives often go up who, rather than come long journeys on horseback would stay at home. When they come to town they must presently be in the mode to get fine clothes, to go to plays and treats, and by these means get such a habit of idleness and love of pleasure as makes them uneasy ever after, and they must have all from London whatever it costs.

Crisset produced figures to back up his argument, and stated that between London and the towns of York, Chester and Exeter, no fewer than eighteen persons travelled by the coaches weekly each way, which came on the whole, to 1,872 passengers in a year!

So the introduction of the stage coach met with objections just as there were objections to the introduction of the railway and the motor car, after which people became more used to innovation in travel methods and protested no more until the sonic boom of Concorde started smashing windows.

Apart from its use on the cart for the carriage of heavy goods, and its adoption as the recoil mechanism of the ships' gun, it was almost as if man had failed to take advantage of the invention of the wheel, and there were some who would have halted its development in the field of transport because when the diligences started running regular services, there was a strong reaction which aimed at returning the British traveller to his right and proper place – the back of a horse.

It was seriously recommended in petitions to the King in Council that no public carriage should be permitted to have more than four horses, to start oftener than once a week, or to go more than thirty miles a day.

It is surprising that the new transport system had become popular enough to arouse opposition at all because Sir Walter Scott spoke of the northern diligence as a "huge old fashioned tub" which was drawn by three horses and in 1745 took three weeks to cover the distance between London and Edinburgh.

It is 1790 before Cumberland comes into the new-fashioned transport picture, and that year "expeditious waggons" were advertised as covering the distance between Carlisle and London in ten days by way of York, leaving Carlisle every Tuesday morning. This early goods transport system foresaw a role for Carlisle which the border city was to fill in the Railway Age as a communications centre, and it promised that from Carlisle goods would be immediately forwarded to Wigton, Cockermouth, Workington and Whitehaven, as well as to Annan, Dumfries, Glasgow, Edinburgh, Aberdeen, "and all other principal towns in Scotland".

The mail coaches came later, "chocolate bodies, picked out with red; the wheels, perch, waist, bars and pole all scarlet, with a royal coat of arms on the panel of the door". They carried four passengers outside and four inside. The mail bags on the roof were in charge of the guard who sat in a seat at the back with a loaded pistol in a pocket on each side of the seat, and a blunderbuss with a load of shot ready to spray on any enterprising highwaymen. The name 'guard', signifying custodianship of the Royal Mail, has persisted into the modern railway system, so has another vital item of the guard's equipment, a reliable timepiece to check that the coach was keeping to its schedule and ensure that stops at the posting houses, where horses where changed and the inner man refreshed, were not overlong. The guard's chronometer also provided a public service in that it was used as a time check on every clock in every stopping place on the route.

Up mails for London left Carlisle at 6 p.m. and reached the capital at 5 o'clock on the second morning, a tiring, muscle-aching, bone-shaking essay in physical endurance which cost the passengers 6 guineas inside, and £3 5*s*. outside, plus extras which were the tips and fees expected by the coachman and guard.

To the modern eye the coaching era presents a picture of 'style', of a quiet, placid way of life when time was unimportant, but time must have been important in a system which could deliver the mail from Carlisle to London in a day and a half.

As coaches proliferated on a road system which was being improved in proportion, it was inevitable that some of the traffic would be aimed at the Lake District whose rise in popularity coincided roughly with the rise of the stage coach.

In 1811 a coaching bill advertised the "Light Post Coach. The Good Intent, From Kendal to Whitehaven" every Tuesday, Thursday and Saturday morning, "at half past five o'clock, by way of Ambleside, Keswick and Cockermouth; Workington to Whitehaven, where it arrives the same evening". Return journeys were on Wednesdays, Fridays and Sundays, connecting with coaches for Manchester and Liverpool.

Principals of this coach service through the heart of the Lakes were John Jackson, of the King's Arms, Kendal; William Wilcock, of the Salutation, Ambleside; John I'Anson,[1] of the Royal Oak, Keswick; and William Wood, of The Globe, Cockermouth, all of them neatly spaced along the route with all the facilities for coaches and passengers.

It is interesting to note that the small print in the bill advertising the 'Good Intent' advised travellers that the operators did not accept responsibility for more than £5 for any damage or loss unless it was declared as being valuable and insured accordingly.

It was a tanner named Banks, who lived at Shu-le-Crow, who started the first coach service from Keswick, as distinct from the regular services which ran through the town. Banks started to run a regular coach to Cockermouth in 1822 by the old road over Whinlatter because the 'new' road (the modern A66) by the side of Bassenthwaite Lake was yet to be built. His coachman was Robert McCade, better known as Bob Kegg, who had the right sort of temperament for the job when other coach services were started and the business became highly competitive. Bob had a quick temper which he took out on both horses and passengers when challenged by a competitor in any of many death-defying races which took place along the tortuous Whinlatter road.

One of the opposition coaches on the same route was driven by Jack Hayes, but Jack's run continued on to Whitehaven. As the demand for more coaches arose, a new line was opened from Keswick to Carlisle, via Bothel and Wigton, with Jack Cowx as the ace driver.

It was Cowx who broke some important new ground in 1824 when he drove the first chaise into Borrowdale. If this does not seem particularly hazardous to modern eyes, it must be remembered that Borrowdale was the valley whose people had infuriated its early visitors by refusing to acknowledge that the wheel had any part to play in their lives, even in their primitive agriculture. The road into Borrowdale was made by and for packhorses, and the danger of the road was underlined when Cowx, expert driver though he was, almost turned the little chaise over at Grange Bridge.[2]

There were accidents. Coaches were turned over by over-enthusiastic drivers trying to keep to schedules. The Over Sands coach from Lancaster became bogged down in soft sand when crossing the Kent estuary at Cartmell in 1811 and was engulfed by the rising tide. Casualties among the fifteen passengers – a large number for a single vehicle, and probably the reason why the coach sank into the sand – included a young lady who was rescued when in danger of being swept away by the racing tide, an old man who was pulled out of the coach and the water "quite senseless", and a woman and her two children who delayed their departure from the doomed coach too long and were swept off the roof before being rescued.[3]

The Lancaster-Keswick-Whitehaven run was the longest served by local coaches, and two of its most famous drivers were Tom Preston and David Johnson, the last of a long line of 'coachees' who stamped their personalities on the Lakes public service vehicles. The journey of 81½ miles usually took 12½ hours and was nearly always completed on time despite the fact that Tom, being an obliging sort of fellow, often undertook to do shopping errands at Keswick or Ambleside for the farm wives on his route.

David Johnson could not do favours for the farm wives because he had to concentrate more on his work, not being as good and as 'natural' a driver as the more experienced Tom, a fact which became obvious when he became involved in perhaps the most spectacular coaching accident in the history of the business in the Lakes.

He might, in fact, have cut short the life of William Wordsworth by some fourteen years, for it was he who drove the coach which in 1856 hit Wordsworth's gig at Rough How bridge on the Ambleside road from Keswick, and "spilled the powett" according to one eye-witness, and ruffled the feathers of the "highly esteemed bard" (as the *Cumberland Pacquet* put it).

The *Pacquet* described the incident thus:

On Wednesday afternoon last between two and three o'clock, as William Wordsworth Esq., the celebrated poet, in company with his son, the Rev. John Wordsworth, of Brigham, were on their way home to Rydal Mount Farm from a visit to the Earl of Lonsdale at Whitehaven Castle, they had a narrow escape from destruction. The venerable and highly esteemed bard and his worthy son were driving in a one-horse gig and had just reached Rough How Bridge,[4] about three miles from Keswick on the Ambleside Road when they observed the mail coach coming upon them at a rattling pace.

Owing to the sharp turn in the road at the top of the ascent which leads down to the bridge, the mail coach could not be seen until within 70 or 80 yards of the place, but in the few moments they had of its approach the Rev. gentleman succeeded in driving his horse close up to the side of the road, which was only narrow, but nevertheless wide enough for the coach to have passed in safety in ordinary circumstances.

It unfortunately happened, however, that the offside wheeler, which, we are told, was in the habit of holding the bridle bit in his teeth, and resisting the utmost exertions of the driver, was at the moment of meeting indulging himself of this dangerous practice, and refusing to obey the rein. Owing to this circumstance the coach came with great violence against the gig, which it sent against the adjoining wall with such force that both the gig and the two riders were thrown, with part of the adjoining wall, into the plantation.

Fortunately the traces and shafts of the gig broke near the body of the vehicle, which set the affrighted animal at liberty, and it no sooner gained its feet than it leaped on the broken wall and having regained the road, set off at a frightened pace with the gig shafts attached to the harness. Such was the affrighted condition of the horse . . . that every attempt to stop it was fruitless, and it dashed on at this furious pace for nearly nine miles, and was eventually stopped at the toll bar entering Grasmere.

Mr Wordsworth and his son . . . were both found entirely unhurt; the only visible injury received by either from this dangerous collision was a slight scratch on the finger of the poet. We do not learn that the slightest blame could be attributed to the driver of the coach who did his utmost to bring the unmanageable animal under his control.

It is on record that when David Johnson was asked about the accident that night and questioned whether Mr Wordsworth was much hurt, he replied: "Nay – but I was nivver mair glad to hear a body swear, for I thowt we'd killed him."

The Westmorland Gazette added its own postscript to a report of the incident: "The accident might easily have proved fatal, and had it done so England would have lost a great figure. We know of no-one who could fill the chasm in society which would have been caused by the heartrending loss of the esteemed and venerated bard of Rydal Mount."

A more colourful account of the smash was delivered at irregular intervals by Jem Arnold, guard on Davy Johnson's coach, when he had, on the encroachment of the railways, retired from the service and taken over as landlord at the Ferry Inn, Windermere. It was ten years after the accident that a contributor to *Frazer's Magazine*, in August 1850, reported Jem Arnold's version. Asked by one of the company staying at the inn if he knew the poet Wordsworth, Jem replied: "Knowed him. I should think I did a few," and rising from his seat he reached and took down a tin horn from beside the beam that ran along the ceiling. "That," said he, eyeing the instrument with a look of affection, "was when I blowed the horn." So saying, he gave a blast that smacked of the coaching days of old.

What the blowing of the horn had to do with his knowing Wordsworth puzzled the company, unused as they were to the native habit, probably inherited from long-forgotten Norse ancestors, of making the simplest of stories into a performance.

Asked to explain, Jem went on: "Why, you see, this is the way I comed to knaw Wadsworth, and I shan't forget in a hurry. When I was guard to the Whitehaven Mail, as we were slapping along and just coming to a sharpish turn, ye knaw the corner by the bridge three miles this side o' Keswick, what should we see but sumthin' tall and grand tooling along a little pony shay as cool as murder. 'Oh! Lor, here's a smash,' says I, and afore the words were out o' mi mouth Crash went the shay all to smithereens, right through a dry wall, and Slap went the driver over into a plantation, arm out and great coat a-flying. We thought for sure it was all over with 'im, but presently he picked hissel up uncommon tall again, and says he, 'I'll have this matter thoroughly investigated.' With that he walked off towards the public" – which would be The

King's Head at Thirlspot – "and 'Jem', said coachee to I, very down like, for 'twas a bad bit o' business, 'who do you think that is?' 'Who! Who!! Davy,' says I, 'Why who but the powit Wadsworth?'

"And now gentlemen," says he, turning round, "when you next go to Keswick, just by the bridge about three miles out, you'll see two yards of the wall down to this day, and that where we spilt the powitt." A prolonged blast on the horn marked the landlord's sense of the excellence of the joke.

"Aye, an' often an' often," he continued, returning the horn to its place, "since that I've seen the grand folks draw up to the Mount, I've said sly to myself, 'Ah, gentlemen, you be a-going to see the powit, but you never had'n call upon you unexpected like, on a flying visit over a wall.' "

Perhaps it was the dawning of an interest in transport which today manifests itself in the mania for collecting relics of the steam railway, but when it became apparent that the stage coach was on its way out, there were 'gentlemen' who took up coaching for coaching's sake.

Such a man was Parson Bird, who lived at Braithwaite Lodge, Keswick, and his special interest was in a coach which ran a service through Keswick and which was called 'The Cuckoo'. So great was this interest that the Parson would ride alongside the coach for miles, watching the horses at work and the coachman manipulating the ribbons. This interest was not altogether without reward for him and benefit for the coachman, for when the driver of 'The Cuckoo' broke a leg in an accident, Parson Bird was able to take over the driving of the coach on its regular run, giving his fees to the crippled coachman.

Coachees who became legends in their lifetime included Jack Taylor, who drove 'The Opposition', an apt name if ever there was one because it was run in opposition to the regular service; Jimmy Telfer, who drove his coach to such fine limits of punctuality that if a passenger was a minute late he would miss it; Tommy Harrison, who renounced his homely Cumbrian dialect and adopted the speech and manner of his more gentle passengers, and cashed in on his ability to do so by amassing a fortune and dying worth £4,000. Hard-living, fast-spending (except for Tommy), they were the gentlemen of the road, and as the railways approached, they found it difficult to relinquish the lives they led, to envisage what life would be without the coaches and horses thundering along the Lakes roads.[5]

Some retired more or less gracefully from the scene, some fought to the bitter end, and one old coachman had what he considered a telling argument against railways which he used time and time again on his passengers. "Don't yer travel by those new fangled steam engines," he cautioned them. "Suppose you travel by my coach and you meets with an accident? There you are! But suppose you travel by rail and you meets an accident? Where are ye?"

When the railways were firmly established – and sufficient reaction to them had set in to scotch the progress of a scheme which would have provided Borrowdale with a railway to carry the Honister slates to Keswick – there began to develop a nostalgia for the horsedrawn coach comparable with the vintage car fancy of today. The Coaching Club and the Four-in-Hand Club were started and it really meant something to belong to one of these prestigious societies.

During the summer of 1881 a Mr Ernest Hargreaves settled in Bowness, acquired a coach – by Holland's, of Lendon – which he named 'The Sportsman', and drove every day from Bowness, via Windermere, to Keswick and back, using in the process a stud of twenty-one horses which were kept in relays at different places along the road.

Hargreaves took on an old professional, Billy Crosthwaite, as co-driver, and set up George Marriner in a red coat to act as guard.

The object of this particular exercise was for Hargreaves to drive sufficient accident-free miles to qualify for membership of the Coaching Club, but he also took fare-paying passengers and did quite well out of it because this route had escaped the railway fever. Unfortunately Hargreaves' health broke down at the end of the first summer, but there were still plenty of coaches running on this route, and they continued to do so until replaced by motor buses.

The Lakes remained as one of the last areas to be served by horsedrawn coaches on a big scale: on such a scale as to make the railways seem quiet and dignified, if we are to believe an American writer who came to the Lakes in 1885.

In the *Pittsburgh Dispatch* of 11 October 1885, E.W. Lighthouse was critical of the heavy coaching traffic met with in the Lakes. After spending the evening listening in The Eagle and Child at Staveley to the local farmers in for refreshment after the haymaking "discoursing on the taxes they had to give to the commonwealth, the clergymen and the capitalist – the three repacious C's which were eating the heart out of the British populace", he slept soundly until: "I was aroused in the morning by the sound of the bugle of a four-in-hand, and directly the coach, loaded to the last seat, dashed past the inn. Then there was another, and another, all carrying gay parties from Kendal to Windermere."

Alter the mode of transport, and things have not changed all that much at Staveley. Lighthouse had come to see the much-vaunted Lakes, but he found Windermere stretching away among the mountains "more like a river than a lake", and the town of Windermere "lying leaden and unlovely among the trees and hills".

On his road to Keswick: "Coaches, coaches everywhere. They gallop at breakneck speed, endangering life and limb. They grind the very rocks of the road into a fine powder, which rises in clouds with every passing breeze. They toot their horns and make a clatter which offends the ear and which causes the hills to cry back at them indignantly. Why", asked E.W. Lighthouse,

> can't these idlers walk or go by cycle? The cycle creeps along on velvet wheels, and as a vehicle of passage is in perfect sympathy with the grand quiet which is the normal condition of these mountains and waters.
>
> But the coaches will thunder on until Gabriel's bugle sounds all the earth into silence.
>
> Here they come down the hill from Kendal, up the hill from Ambleside, blue, brown, black and buff coaches; black horses and white, gay horses and gray; coachmen and footmen in scarlet livery; coachmen and footmen in blue livery; coachmen and footmen in plum-coloured livery; buglers blowing the blood all into their faces and fairly bursting their cheeks. Crack, crack;

crack, snap, go a dozen coachmen's dozen whips as coach follows coach coming in style from all directions to the fashionable hotels; gallop, gallop, gallop go the horses just as though they had not galloped for miles; the coaches swerve from side to side; so some of the passengers sing, some laugh, some scream. Timid outsiders imagine the top-heavy thing is going over, and hang on to the rails and seats for dear life. There is a race to see who will first reach the hotels in view, for there is doubt about rooms, and each coachman desires to favour his passengers. "Hey, hey, hey! G'long, g'long, g'long" shout some of the drivers; and with clatter and swing, and rumble and roar, roar, that's how the coaches come down from Lo . . . But no, we will not have Lodore yet.[6]

Just before the dawn of the motor age, the Lakes suffered the real dark of the coaching age, but many more years were to pass before coaching ended in the district and well into the twentieth century coaches still ran, and wagonettes, serving the hotels: picking up guests at Lakeside, Keswick and Penruddock and taking them into the inner fastnesses of this lovely area which had resisted total penetration by the railways.

It is not so very long ago that the wagonettes lined up in Keswick Market Place, their attendants touting for custom for trips over Honister, which is the nearest a Lakeland amusement ever got to Blackpool's 'Big Dipper' and on which those passengers who were able to do so had to walk up the steepest bits, a chore more than compensated for by the thrill of riding down with the brakes screeching and the drag rasping over the uneven surface of the road.[7]

Old coachees helped to run the coaches and wagonettes for the hotels, or went into business: into innkeeping like Jem Arnold, or, like John Lewthwaite, emigrated to the New World where stage coaches were still a part of the way of life although, even out in the Far West, in decline at the advance of the railroads.

And when the steam locomotive had taken over, and horse carriages lingered only on the roads up Borrowdale and into Patterdale and other such remote places, there were many men who could echo Lewthwaite when, from Canada, he wrote:

I saw myself perched on the old coach again,
The ribbons of four topping bays in my hands,
And tooting a thrilling old coaching refrain,
That rang through the vales of that glorious land.

4

The Undoing of Pigtail Armstrong

'Aback o' Warnell Fell leaves a Bewcastle tyke;
For dealing i' horseflesh, theer niver was sek like.
Bit a'tween twea deed hosses theer nut much t'choose,
An' Askew bet Pigtail be t'hide an' fower shoes.'

That is not the best verse ever written in the Cumberland dialect. It is not good verse; it is not even in good dialect. It has, however, served a valuable purpose in putting on record a horse-trading incident which has become part of Cumbrian folklore.

The trouble with folklore, which is usually based on historical fact, is that sometimes in the telling and re-telling of the tale the original set of facts becomes fogged, which is why these four lines of poetry of questionable merit are important: they are a genuine historical record, and they put the record straight – in favour of that Cumbrian hunting hero, John Peel.

Poor old John Peel had a far from unstained character. Although there were no complaints in his lifetime, his critics have said that he drank too much, he devoted too much time to hunting and too little to his family and farm, and, in fact, spent a lifetime demonstrating what a good Cumbrian 'statesman' farmer and family man should not be.

But he did not, as at least two of his biographers have said he did, take any part in a horse-cowping deal in which he 'did' the other party in the deal out of the animal's hide and four shoes.

A horse-cowper John Peel certainly was; he had to be if he was his father's son, and his frequent visits to Rosley Hill Fair show that he retained this interest most of his life. And, again if he was following in his father's example, he was a 'gey honest yin', for old William Peel always allowed any horses he sold out 'on trial' before a deal was concluded.

The credit – if that is the correct word – for the 'doing' of Pigtail Armstrong belongs, as that bit of old dialect doggerell says, to Askew Peel, John Peel's young brother.

John Peel was the eldest of a large family; Askew was twelve years younger . . . at least he was christened in 1789, twelve years after John was baptised. Askew lived at Caldbeck, and among his drinking companions was Willie Armstrong, a scion of the old Border reiving clan from Bewcastle Fells. Descended from a family which kept the Border Troubles alive long after the Acts of Union of 1707 were supposed to have stopped them, Willie retained a dishonest streak. This came out in the way he got his nickname 'Pigtail'. It was said that he was engaged in a pigstealing exploit which came unstuck when the alarm was raised, and Pigtail was left holding only the tail of the animal he had come to steal.

Askew and Pigtail had a running argument about the value of their respective horses, and whenever they met, usually on Sundays in the inn at Caldbeck, the fun would start and all the locals present would sit back and listen. Pigtail had an old mare called Fanny, and Askew had an equally aged steed called Blossom. There wasn't a toss of difference between the two nags, and current opinion in a district which was knowledgeable about horseflesh was that, both together, they might, with a bit of luck and a half-blind customer, have fetched twenty-five or thirty shillings at Rosley Fair.

So Askew and Pigtail would set to work and try and sell their horses to each other, or to organize a swap which would be mutually acceptable, and they had been at it so long that the locals had given up hope that there ever would be a deal between the two. It didn't stop them trying, or make the arguments any the less interesting, because Cumbrian pubs have ever been venues for the endless joke.

One Thursday morning Askew went for Blossom and found her lying stone dead in a gutter at the bottom of his croft. He told nobody of his discovery. In the afternoon, with a mug of ale at his elbow, Askew was sitting in the Rising Sun when in walked Pigtail Armstrong. There were the usual preliminaries. Pigtail bought his ale, they mentioned the weather, and gradually Askew turned the conversation to the old topic: a trade of their mares.

Pigtail said he would swop his Fanny for Askew's Blossom and five shillings.

"Nivver," said Askew, who said that his Blossom was five shillings better than Fanny. The haggling continued, and, to the astonishment of the listeners, the gap between the two offers began to close. And at long last the two settled on a bargain – a straight swop. Pigtail agreed to deliver Fanny that evening.

By evening the village was agog. News travelled fast. Not only did everybody know that a deal had been finalized, but they also knew now that Askew had sold Pigtail Armstrong a dead horse. They awaited the outcome with interest.

A small crowd had collected on the street leading to Askew's when Pigtail arrived that evening driving a flat cart with Fanny lying on it, dead as a doornail. Pigtail's anxiety to complete a deal was now explained. The cart wended a slow, jerking way down the village street, a swarm of youngsters tailing on behind to see the fun and making Pigtail's job of driving rather difficult by shouting "Whoaaa" about every five yards. As the recorder of the event[2] said: "T'oald hoss in t' shafts was varra tractable; it stop't aboot ivvery time it was tell't."

Smiling smugly, Pigtail halted the cart at Askew's front door. "Noo, Askew me lad! Whoar'll te hev her?"

Askew did not bat an eyelid when he came out and saw what Pigtail had brought. Pointing to the stable end, he said: "Just towp her up theer."

Pigtail did as he was told and tipped the dead Fanny to the ground.

Straight-faced, Askew led his old friend to the croft where Blossom lay. But she had been stripped of both hide and shoes – all that was of any value about a dead horse.

That score off Pigtail Armstrong was considered to be

worth the attention of some local bard who composed the lines which lead off this chapter, and which were often sung to one of the hunting song tunes.

The words lack the style of 'D'ye ken John Peel?' and so it had a brief vogue in the lifetime of its characters and then disappeared into the limbo of forgotten things to be revived when 'Young' John Peel, the hunter's eldest son, was eighty years old and reminiscing about the good old days for a *West Cumberland Times* reporter.

5

A Sacrifice to Forestry

Ennerdale is the quietest, least frequented of the western valleys of the Lake District. It has also suffered greater changes than any of the other valleys.

In forty years the valley, from Bowness Knott up to the Scarth Gap-Black Sail track, has undergone a complete change of face and character. In the process, and because of it, Ennerdale has come under more public notice than any of the others because of the demands made upon it, by the Forestry Commission for tree-planting, by Whitehaven for lake water.

The Anglers' Hotel which once stood at the Lakeside has been swept away,[1] and the entire valley floor eastwards from Bowness Knott is all forest trees.

It was, perhaps, the Ennerdale experience which gave the National Park authority the leverage necessary to draw from the Forestry Commission a covenant that there would be no more such forestry operations in the central area of the National Park. Certainly plans for large-scale afforestation in the Hardknott area where shelved rather hurriedly.

Forty years ago the Birketts raised Herdwicks at Gillerthwaite, but now that ancient Ennerdale farm is a hostel, and the road to it has a bar across at Bowness Knott which says "authorized vehicles only". The unspoken order is "this is where you get out and walk", and to underline the point, the Forestry Commission has provided a car park and picnic area and gone to some trouble to mark out nature trails in woodland which was once open fell.

In the early 1930s bikes or cars could be left in the care of the Birketts and after a short walk up the valley the turbulent

Liza could be crossed where it shallowed at a wire fence. This fence led to a high-level route which fetched up beside Pillar Rock's western face where a clear spring of ice-cold water issued from among the rocks – ideal refreshment before starting a rock climb. It was a gentle gradient to Pillar that, a way which could be covered at a speed fitting the impatience of youth, and a route so well known that one night a friend ran all the way back from Liza to the Pillar spring in total darkness to retrieve a missing torch.

Then one day after crossing the Liza and starting the climb up by the fence, there was a man busy with a spade turning over clods of the peaty soil of the fell and in each clod planting a miniature fire tree.

"You're trespassing, hop it!" he said, and one era had ended and another had begun in Ennerdale. The route to Pillar from then on would be that dreadful haul up a forest ride.

Those miniature fir trees have grown, been thinned; some probably harvested as mature timber, and similar conifers have spread over the valley, although the natural woodlands on the southern shore of the lake remain.

It is difficult to decide whether the Ennerdale experience has been good or bad. There are probably more visitors now than there have ever been, and the Forestry Commission employ more people than ever made a living on Ennerdale farms; there are still no shops, ice-cream parlours or telephone lines . . . and the road to Gillerthwaite is still only good in parts, and not completely enveloped in trees.

Ennerdale was quite unspoiled and now it is a forest planted with profit in mind, but still it rations itself to visitors by its poor access roads. The Anglers' road, pitted and potholed, goes over a field, and the road down to the car park at Bowness Knott is even less of a motorists' delight than the Watendlath road. It would be an ideal place for the Lake District Planning Board to carry out a traffic management experiment comparable with that operating in the Peak District's Goyt Valley, but there is not yet a great deal of traffic to manage. Strange as it may sound in these days of complaints about 'crowded' Lakeland, Ennerdale has not yet been 'discovered'. When it is the Forestry Commission will be held to have done a fine job with their nature trails and some of their roadside planting. There cannot be any complaints from anyone who did not know Ennerdale as it used to be.[2]

There was a time when one of the seasonal attractions was Char Dub in the River Liza near where it enters the lake, and if the season was wintry Martinmas people went there just the same to see the lake's entire char[3] population congregated in the Dub for the spawning.

One who was attracted over the fells to see the char at spawning time was Dr David Lietch, of Keswick. In his notebook dated Wednesday 25 November 1850,[4] Dr Lietch reported: "Went over to Ennerdale to see the spawning char of that lake, which, I was told run up in Martinmas Week, and remain a fortnight, and deposit their spawn in 'The Char Dub'."

Experienced char fishermen like Tyson of Buttermere, and Jopson of Crummock Lake, had assured Lietch that he was wasting his time: that it was too late in the season; that the char would have all gone down. Lietch and two companions arrived at Gillerthwaite when they were sheep-salving. The Gillerthwaite salve must have been sweeter than most because its smell did not drive them away, and they remained to partake of Gillerthwaite hospitality, freely given:

> an immense platter of baked flesh and a mountainous pile of mashed potatoes . . . while in the metal pan on the fire, covered with a metal lid on which was heaped red embers forming the usual oven of the mountains, the mighty remains of an apple pie being heated up.
>
> Cheese upon the upper shelves near to the rafters, and hooks for hanging goodly supplies of bacon . . . a fireplace ornamented with circular projections of stone, whereon to deposit kettles or pans, and a crew of shepherds' dogs lying about the stone floor . . .

Refreshed, the visitors sallied forth

> by the little river side, circled by the grand snowy mountains – the Pillar, the Steeple, Red Pike, and the dark walls of an abrupt high land that shut in the gleaming steel mirror of Ennerdale

Lake, a most magnificent winter scene.

About three hundred yards above the lake, where a stone wall runs down to the river is a long "dub" or pool, one part of which is very deep.

This was the famous Ennerdale Char Dub, and the char had not yet gone back to the lake, the dub was black with thousands of the little fish.

Needing a couple of the fish for an artist friend to paint, Lietch tried a bent pin with a piece of red rag as bait, but the char had other things on their minds, so the doctor and his friends "took other means" to drive the fish downstream and scoop out a few by hand.

"Small as they looked in the water," wrote Lietch,

> yet they were occasionally as large as Buttermere char. One or two were eight ounces . . . most resplendently coloured, red and gold bellied, fins with a pink shade in the centre, shaded into a brown ash blue and edged with pearl colour . . . a most brilliant and elegant creature, wanting however, the regular white spots which add so much to the beauty of the Buttermere char.

Ennerdale char still spawn in the Liza although the famous Dub is now filling up with stones and gravel, but environmentalists may find some consolation in the fact that although Dr Lietch found the biggest char in the Dub to be of eight ounces, Ennerdale char today run up to two pounds in weight.

The Anglers', a famous hostel in its day, was named for the people who went there for the fishing, but now its site is a car park and picnic area. On the way there from Ennerdale Bridge the road passes a massive barn-like structure which seems at odds with the usual run of Lakes architecture. And so it is, for this is The How – also known at various times in its long history as How Hall and Caswell Hall – once the home of the Patricksons, a powerful family of the neighbourhood in the sixteenth century, and a stone in the wall declares that "This house was built A.D. 1566 by Anthony Patrickson, and Frances, his wife, the daughter of Sir Thomas Swinburne, one of the Privy Council to Henry VIII."

There are other stones about which are relics of the Old

Hall of the Patricksons, but perhaps the most important memento of this family is the reputation they earned for litigation among themselves and with others which whittled away the family's fortunes.

The Anthony Patrickson who built the Hall started it when, as lord of the manors of Loweswater, Thackthwaite, Whinfell and Dean, he tried to assert his new-found authority by infringing the rights of his tenants. They held their land under the system of customary tenancy which meant that, in exchange for privileges which included paying low rents, they were obliged to be at readiness to serve in the Border wars. An armed tenantry in an area whose ownership was constantly in dispute with the kings of Scotland was a valuable attribute to the Crown.

However, Patrickson, feeling that some of the heat was being taken out of the Border situation, in 1597 arbitrarily increased the rents of his tenants without consulting either them or the Crown.

Jealous of their rights, the tenants of Loweswater took the matter in a Bill of Complaint to the High Court of Chancery, stating that

> they and their assigns had time out of mind been seised to them and their heirs according to the ancient and laudable custom of tenant right within the west marches of England, and about fifty years since did hold the same of the late King Henry VIII by the said custom, and by paying a certain yearly rent and fine certain at the death of the lord and the death of the tenant. Further holding their several tenements by service·on the said borders of England over against Scotland of their own proper costs and charged within ye said west marches when and so often as thereto they shall be required by the lord warden . . .

The tenants won their case, and Patrickson lost both rents and face, but he was a litigious fellow and he and his heirs so spent their wealth until The How was sold to the Tiffin family in the seventeenth century.

Patricksons remained in the district, however, and in the parish register it is noted that on 14 March 1681, Thomas Patrickson of Stockhow was "wrapped and buried in woollen". This was in accord with an Act of Parliament of

1667 which, to encourage the woollen trade, decreed that no material should be used in the burial of a body except wool.

The Patricksons rose and fell, the Tiffins came and went, the Tysons came to Gillerthwaite and left, and so did the last of the Gillerthwaite flockmasters, the Birketts. Today summer visitors come and go in smaller numbers than to any other Lakeland valley, and the char still emerge from the icy depths of the steel-grey lake at Martinmas to spawn in the Liza beck cold from the melt-water of the first winter snows. Trees are planted, are thinned and felled, and above the tree-line everything is almost as it has always been.

Pillar, for instance. This great mass of rock, riven by vertical cracks and gullies so that it looks like the nightmare of a drunken architect trying to design a Gothic cathedral with a broken pencil on disintegrating paper, is the rock-climber's Mecca. Other crags have their devotees – Dow, Gimmer, the Napes and Kern Knotts on Great Gable, Scafell – but for so many Pillar is *the* rock above all other Lakeland rocks, and the pillarite who has climbed all its multitude of routes is indeed a man of distinction.

This venerable pile of rock looks serenely down on the forests which have been planted and grown and will be harvested in only a minute fraction of its lifetime, and across to the industrial west of Cumbria whence many of its climbers have come, beckoned by the outline of the rock which, in silhouette, looks like the vast stone chair for an even vaster stone statue.

Pillar has a sort of privacy in that it is off the mainstream beaten tracks. It takes considerable effort to get there whether the approach is from Ennerdale and up the wide forestry 'ride', from Wasdale and the Black Sail summit along the High Level Route, or from Buttermere via Scarth Gap. With this sort of isolation, Pillar is seldom crowded, and its climbers seldom find themselves performing before a gallery as they do on the Napes, Kern Knotts, Borrowdale's Shepherd's Crag, or Scafell's mighty buttresses.

Pillar Rock has its own place in the histories of the dale because for ages its top was untrodden by man, an Everest among Lakeland tops until, in 1826, a young shepherd called Atkinson (or Aitchison, which is a Cumbrian way of pronouncing the name, and which has become a family surname in its own right) reached the top of the Rock and became officially the first man to climb Pillar.

Some doubt has been thrown on Atkinson's claim by William Wordsworth, who in 'The Brothers', written in 1800, suggests that there was an earlier ascent than Atkinson's. Topographically, Wordsworth can seldom be faulted in either his prose of his poetry, all his locations being easily identifiable to this day. And so it was in 'The Brothers'. There can be no doubt that he is writing about Pillar Rock and not Pillar Mountain when his priest of Ennerdale speaks of:

> . . . yon precipice; – it wears the shape
> Of a vast building made of many crags;
> And in the midst is one particular rock
> That rises like a column from the vale,
> Whence by our shepherds it is called The Pillar.

Again, Wordsworth did not often invent situations, people and events, and if he did tend to overdo his Arcadian view of the Lakes, the people he writes about are real enough.

It would be fair, then, to assume that when in 'The Brothers' he writes about the death of James Ewbank, the younger, stay-at-home brother, in a fall from Pillar, he records an actual event, and, therefore, an earlier ascent of Pillar than that credited to Atkinson.

Wordsworth wrote about young Ewbank, lagging behind his companion shepherds in going the rounds of their sheep

> . . . among the new-dropped lambs

lay down to rest, fell asleep, started to walk in his sleep – an affliction for which he had been noted – and fell down the Rock to his death.

> They found him at the foot of that same rock
> Dead and with mangled limbs.

The Rock is clearly identified as the location of the tragedy, but getting to the summit of Pillar Rock was unlikely to be part of the usual round of Ennerdale shepherds. The fall might have been from the more accessible Low Man, from

Sham Rock, or even down Walker's Gully out of the Amphitheatre.

However, the 'tragedy' leaves in its wake a piece of Pillar lore which Wordsworth re-tells:

> . . . when the youth
> Fell, in his hand he must have grasped, we think,
> His shepherd's staff; for on that Pillar of rock
> It had been caught mid-way; and there for years
> It hung and mouldered there.

The story of the young shepherd's staff was handed down to generations of climbers by the Ennerdale farmers, and there were hundreds of them who half expected that one day they would find it, or remains of it still hanging, still mouldering there . . . somewhere in the vicinity of the North Climb was regarded as the most likely area. The cracks, chimneys, aretes, slabs, buttresses of Pillar have been so well explored that it would have been difficult to overlook even the ferrule of that shepherd's staff – if it was ever there.

The shepherd's story and the shepherd's staff go into Pillar's folklore, which, when we examine the matter closely, is probably where Wordsworth got it from in the first place because diligent search of the Ennerdale parish registers prior to 1800 reveals nothing about any Ewbank buried in the parish churchyard, and the records of the Coroners for the Lordship of Egremont have no mention of any inquest on any Ewbank being killed at Pillar, or anywhere else.

The first ascent of Pillar Rock was probably by the Old West route, which is certainly the easiest way, but it weaves a labyrinthine way up the face which in the virgin state of the Rock would be difficult to find, or retrace. A few generations of eager climbers have made the route, and many more of the easier climbs, much more visible with heavy boots clawing the rock with ring-clinkers, tricounis, and a variety of other climbing hardware which came under the common title of 'nails'.

The easy Slab and Notch route could have been an early way to the top of the Rock, and the likelihood must not be disregarded that one day a brave spirit took the shortest way up and reached the top by way of what is now known as the Central Jordan climb.

Soon, climbing Pillar Rock became a prestigious achievement, and by 1874 there was a bottle on top in which visitors left their cards or pieces of paper on which they had written their names.

Two years later a couple of men described as 'navvies' went to the top and took away the bottle and all it contained in the way of mementoes of the conquerors of the Rock. These included something left by Miss A. Barker, the first woman to climb the Rock, on 9 July 1870; and a handkerchief left by Miss Mary Westmorland of Penrith in 1874, the second lady to the top. Miss Edith Maitland and a Miss Butler went up in 1875. In the same year Mrs Ann Crears was the first married woman to climb Pillar.

The bottle was replaced by a brass canister with a screw lid, but that also disappeared despite being chained to the rock.

Pillar, discovered, became a target for intrepid pioneers of the rock-climbing cult, with W.P. Hasket-Smith in the van, and eventually sufficient routes had been climbed on the Rock to merit it being given its own guide-book by the Fell and Rock Climbing Club, routes with names like Curtain and Arete, Central Jordan, New West, the North Climb, Savage Gully, South West, Route I and Route II, and The Appian Way . . . very few climbs named after the people who pioneered them, as if the very character of Pillar defied anybody to annexe even a climbing route in his own name.

It was not that the Pillar was short of personalities among its devotees. One of the more remarkable was the Rev. James Jackson, of Sandwith, whose association with the Rock was short, but remarkably sweet.

He first reached the top of Pillar in 1875 when he was seventy-nine. Three years later he set off from Wasdale Head for Pillar and went missing. His body was found on Great Doup, and in his haversack was a bottle intended as a replacement for the one the navvies had taken. In the bottle was a piece of paper on which he had written the following:

Two elephantine properties are mine,

Skiddaw from Whinlatter

The Southey memorial in Crosthwaite church

Windermere from the Low Wood Inn, one of the old coaching hostelries on the Kendal-Keswick run, from an engraving by Thomas Allom

Windermere from Ferry House, from an engraving by Thomas Allom

The 'old' road up Borrowdale, now the footpath to the Bowder Stone

Rough How Bridge, now disused, where Wordsworth came to grief in collision with the stage coach

Ennerdale from How Hall, from an engraving by Thomas Allom

The modern farmhouse at The How, Ennerdale. The older building, probably occupied by the Patricksons, now a barn, can be seen in the background

No salmon river this! The Derwent above Grange-in-Borrowdale

Ennerdale Water from the site of the old Anglers' Inn

The Char Dub at Ennerdale

For I can bend to pick up pin or plack,
And when this year the Pillar Rock I climb,
Fourscore years and two's the howdah on my back.

Jackson had given himself the title 'Patriarch of the Pillar' and in the happily exclusive brotherhood of climbing which then existed, he had playfully appointed John Maitland 'Patriarch Presumptive', a title which Maitland took seriously enough to undertake the job of placing a cairn with a cross where Jackson's body had been found.

Less spectacular was the death of Edward Barnard, a London goldsmith, who was bitten by the laking bug and laid down to die near Pillar in 1876, and also had a cairn erected to his memory. Fortunately the building of cairns to the memory of people who died in the Lake Country went out of fashion, otherwise the Lakes today – or parts of it – would look something like an Egyptian graveyard.

They erected no cairn to the memory of Thomas Walker, a 17-year-old apprentice from Whitehaven, who was killed on Good Friday 1883, but his memorial is more substantial, more lasting than any cairn, because he slipped on a rock in the Amphitheatre and fell down the Rock's most famous cleft which now bears his name – Walker's Gully.

6

Accident, or ...?

When any aged Cumbrian introduced into a conversation the words "Ah've heer't tell . . ." it was usually the preamble to the relation of a bit of local lore which, based on truth as most of it was – or outright fiction, was bound to be interesting.

But sometimes the truth was so distorted by telling and re-telling of the tale that it was difficult to categorize any story as fact or fable.

Such a story, "o' lang sen", is that of the Ouse Bridge incident which is more often than not dismissed as fable because it has in it so many of the ingredients of the sort of melodrama which was popular in Victorian times.

This is a story, however, in which the truth is stranger than the fictions which have been wound around it by old wives in their frequent re-tellings.

Ouse Bridge, scene of the story, spans the Derwent where that wonderfully clear river leaves Bassenthwaite Lake. Built in 1810, and very little altered since, it is one of the loveliest of Cumbrian bridges, and certainly stands in the most picturesque of settings. It is a bridge which was built when nobody could see far enough into the future to envisage a time when two vehicles going in opposite directions might meet on the bridge, so it was built, and remains, wide enough for only one vehicle, whether stage coach, farm cart or modern motor car.

Its fame rests on other things than its beauty or the beauty of its setting. It spans the river over the redds where the salmon spawn, and was for many years a sort of promised land for poachers, who using a variety of 'illegal machines and instruments', took out salmon by the cartload.[1]

It was also the scene, on 28 June 1832, of an incident which has never been fully explained.

John Martin was the son of a prosperous farmer of Shatton, near Cockermouth, and he struck up a friendship with Mary Armstrong of Cockermouth, a dressmaker. The friendship blossomed and, as often happened in days when parental approval for marriages of young men below the age of twenty-six or twenty-seven was difficult to obtain, John got Mary, as they said, "into trouble".

Mary, considering that she had made quite a good catch in netting John, was delighted. John was not quite so enthralled as he might have been, and his parents considered that he had chosen a mate a long way beneath his station in life.

However, there is a hint of Mary's father hovering menacingly in the background with a shotgun, and eventually it was agreed that Mary and John should be married.

Cockermouth being what it was, the news soon spread around, and it was generally agreed that Mary had made an excellent catch, although there were some who felt that John had been trapped.

The banns were called, and there were no objectors in Cockermouth's All Saints Church, and the couple were "hinging in t' bell reaps"[2] as the local saying went, when it was decided that Mary would go and stay with John's uncle at Bassenthwaite until their wedding day the following Saturday.

With the hay to get in, John worked hard on the Shatton farm all day, and it was midnight before he called for Mary at her home. He was riding a horse, and with Mary riding pillion, they made slow but steady progress towards Bassenthwaite.

On reaching Ouse Bridge John stopped his horse and, saying there was something wrong with the saddle, dismounted. According to Mary's story, John was pretending to put his saddle right when he suddenly siezed her by the legs and threw her over the bridge and into the swollen River Derwent, and then remounted his horse and rode off.

Mary did not make it clear whether John threw her over the bridge from the back of the horse, or whether she was sitting on the parapet of the bridge when John siezed her legs and 'towped' her into the river below.

John's version was that she was standing on the low parapet wall preparing to remount the horse when she overbalanced and fell, her scream frighting the horse so that it ran away with him.

John completed his journey to Bassenthwaite and reported his loss.

Mary, who had fallen more than twenty feet into the river, which was running high, received little injury and struggled to the river bank downstream where, exhausted, she waited until four o'clock and then set off to walk to the house of a friend in Embleton.

If it was a genuine accident, John made no attempt at rescue, and did not report it at the nearest house which would be the inn which stood near the bridge and which Sir William Fletcher Vane, of Armathwaite Hall, had had built "for the convenience of travellers". Neither did he report it at any of the several houses which lay between Ouse Bridge and Bassenthwaite Haws, but his excuse for that was that the horse had bolted with him on it.

And why did Mary linger for something like three hours at the riverside before going to see her friends in Embleton? There were several places of call on the way where she could have reported the incident. Was she afraid that John, having already attempted to murder her, would come downstream to make sure that the job had been well done?

Mary went into the police house at Cockermouth the following day and laid her complaint. She also made a statement about the incident which was taken down by the constable, but when he asked her to sign it she refused to do so!

This placed the constable in a dilemma. A complaint had been laid, and a charge had been made, and even if Mary had refused to sign it, something had to be done. John Martin was arrested and put before the local magistrates, who, despite the fact that she had not signed it, heard the statement she had made read out by the constable. The justices asked Mary if she would sign her statement, and she refused. The magistrates, in a dilemma themselves now, committed John to the local lock-up.

In the meantime things were moving between the Armstrong and Martin families. There were discussions, John was visited in the lock-up, and now, as the only way of saving his skin, made it clear that he wished to marry Mary.

Then John came before the Cockermouth magistrates again, and again Mary refused to sign the statement she had made. The magistrates lost patience and committed both Mary and John to the House of Correction in St Helens Street.

On 9 July they were again brought before the magistrates and Mary again refused to sign. So John was committed to Carlisle Gaol to take his trial at the approaching Assizes. Mary was bound over to appear to give evidence against him.

The case had excited the interest of the whole county, but the *Cumberland Pacquet* was sceptical and in its issue of 10 July wrote: "The romantic nature of the tale has caused considerable doubts in the minds of many as to the veracity of the girl's statement."

Which drew an indignant reaction from the Cockermouth magistrates, men of standing and property whose words and actions were not to be treated lightly. The following week the *Pacquet* stated: " . . . in our last . . . we expressed some doubt as to the veracity of the girl's story, which was undoubtedly one of a singularly romantic nature. We have since been given to understand that the evidence on which Martin was committed was perfectly satisfactory to every one who heard it."

Unwittingly, however, the Cockermouth magistrates had condemned John Martin to a particularly unpleasant death. A cholera plague, which decimated the populations of towns in Cumbria, was raging at the time, and it found an excellent breeding place in Carlisle goal. The *Cumberland Pacquet* of 7 August 1832 reported: "John Martin, the man accused of throwing his sweetheart over Ouse Bridge, near Cockermouth, with intent to drown her, died of cholera in

Carlisle gaol last week. This unfortunate individual was attacked with the fatal malady on Tuesday and died the following day. Two other cases in the gaol also terminated fatally."

What became of Mary Armstrong is not known; what the truth of the matter was cannot be told either, because all the information available is what was reported of the hearings before the magistrates. John Martin's story was never officially heard; Mary's story was not put to the test.

If John had survived to stand trial, Mary would surely have had to give evidence and, if found guilty, he would have been transported to Botany Bay or Tasmania. Most interesting, if it could be told, would be what John's reactions were when he discovered that Mary was alive and well and living in Cockermouth.

The 'old wives' tale' of the Ouse Bridge incident said that Martin and Mary were on their way to a party when Mary was thrown over the bridge. John then went on to the party, the idea being that he would ask where Mary was and express surprise that she had not already arrived. However, this version said that when John got to the party, Mary was already there, looking at him accusingly.

The old story never got beyond that; the old-time story-tellers liked to end on a high note.

7

Salmon – The Great Initiative

Above Grange-in-Borrowdale, the River Derwent looks like every angler's dream: the classic river, abounding, one would believe, in trout and salmon awaiting the opportunity to snap at a fisherman's lure.

Here, however, apperances are deceptive. It is not a good river for the dedicated angler: dedicated, that is, to catching fish. For thrashing the water in the cosy glow of a summer day for the angler not so dedicated to catching fish there is, perhaps, no better place on earth.

The angler will catch the odd trout perhaps; very infrequently a small salmon, but more often than not there is only an empty basket and an enduring memory of time spent in matchless surroundings.

In short, the Borrowdale Derwent is not an anglers' river.

This is strange because the mainstream Derwent and its major tributaries rate among the best salmon-fishing water in England, and at first sight there seems little to choose between any of those tributaries – the Marron entering the Derwent at Bridgefoot, the Cocker at Cockermouth, or the Greta at Keswick – and the headwaters of the Derwent proper in Borrowdale. They are all fast, turbulent streams of clear water with feeders which seem ideal spawning ground for the king of fish – in fact have all those physical characteristics which salmon requires of its home water.

The trouble with the Borrowdale Derwent is that there are times when its exuberance is tantamount to violence; when its water stops rippling and starts to roar, turns flow into flood. And when the Borrowdale Derwent goes into flood, fed by the high rainfall of the surrounding fells, which at times can beat the Indian monsoon at its own game, the river and its feeders rage through the valley like horizontal Niagaras.

Salmo salar may have its moments of foolishness in falling for 'flies' which look like anything but flies, but it is very discriminating in its choice of spawning places, and a river which can rise and spread the boulders out of its bed into the surrounding fields and produce a force equivalent to scores of bulldozers at full power, is hardly the place to offer a nice smooth bank of pebbles for a spawning redd with any guarantee that either spawn or redd will be there after the first autumnal storm.

Salmon deposit their spawn in the quieter becks where the eggs will mature and hatch, and, when hatched, will give the alevins at least Mother Nature's thousand-to-one chance of survival to the fingerling stage.

The sudden outburst of flood temper displayed by the Borrowdale Derwent would fling ova, fry or parr headlong into Derwentwater and into the welcoming maws of that beautiful lake's ravenous pike.

For want of any better reason, that is why the salmon do not use the Borrowdale Derwent as a spawning river, and, since salmon only ascend a river to spawn, it is the reason why salmon are seldom found in it.

There was a time when men with fishing on their minds thought differently: that the Derwent's lack of salmon was due to some aberration on Nature's part, and that all that was required to correct this mistake was a nudge in the right direction.

Such a man was a Dr Parnaby, an off-comer who lived at Newton Place which stands opposite the Borrowdale Hotel.

It is difficult to judge whether it was he or a Mr J.J. Armistead who founded the fish hatchery in Troutdale, but though Armistead certainly ran part of the business as a salmon hatchery, it was Parnaby who took the great initiative which was to lead to a solution of part of the mystery of the Atlantic salmon.

Troutdale is an offshoot of Borrowdale, hidden from most

people who pass that way 'doing' the Lakes; known to walkers who take this route up Grange Fell for spectacular views of Borrowdale; familiar to several generations of rock climbers who have gone there to clamber up Black Crag Buttress, which is also known as Troutdale Pinnacle, and which was one of Borrowdale's very few 'listed' climbs until pioneers like Bentley Beetham, exploring Borrowdale's rocks, opened up a whole new world for the cragsmen.

The name 'Troutdale' poses a question similar to the classic "Which came first: the chicken or the egg?" Whether it was Troutdale before or only after the hatchery was set up is a matter for conjecture, but because there is no record of a 'Troutdale' as a Borrowdale offshoot earlier than the hatchery experiment, it can be assumed that the name was conjured out of the purpose for which the little dale was used more than a century ago.

It was some time before 1860 that the Troutdale fish hatchery was built. It consisted of a stone building in which the hatchery was situated, the fish eggs being held on trays of glass rods in troughs of running water fed from the little stream which runs down the valley.[1] Then there was the rearing shed, a huge tarred-timber building erected to protect the rearing tanks which were deep cement-lined troughs at ground level in which the larger fish were kept, and the tanks for the newly hatched fish which were waterproofed wooden troughs at waist level above the rearing tanks. The whole system was so arranged that a continuous supply of fresh mountain water flowed through every tank.

The idea of pisciculture was, of course, not new; men have been running fish farms of various sorts as long as history has been recorded. Troutdale's aim was not to raise fish for the table, but to sell to people wishing to stock or restock rivers, lakes and ponds. It was a great success, and in fifteen years, by which time it was owned by Armistead, the business had outgrown its premises, and Armistead found a new base of operations at New Abbey in Dumfriesshire.

For a time he continued to operate the Troutdale hatchery, and his catalogue of fish available, mostly as 'eyed' ova but

PRICE LIST OF OVA (IN QUANTITY.)

SALMONIDÆ.

All eggs are sent out when *fully-eyed* unless specially desired otherwise. It is the latest stage at which they can be removed with safety, and they usually hatch in a very short time after arrival at their destination.

The following are the present **PRICES FOR FINE HEALTHY "FULLY-EYED" EGGS** of **TROUT**, including **Brown Trout, Yellow Trout, Anglo-Swiss Trout, Buttermere Trout, Loch Kindar Trout, Loch Leven Trout, American Trout, Fario x Levenensis** or **Levenensis x Fario Hybrids,** any of which are delivered **carriage paid** and **carefully packed** to any railway station in Britain :—

100,000	**selected ova**	**£30**	**0s.**	**0d.**
50,000	**do.**	**£16**	**10s.**	**0d.**
20,000	**do.**	**£7**	**10s.**	**0d.**
15,000	**do.**	**£6**	**0s.**	**0d.**
10,000	**do.**	**£4**	**0s.**	**0d.**
5,000	**do.**	**£2**	**5s.**	**0d.**

Special Quotations on Application for Export Orders.

The most economical method of stocking is by laying down **fully-eyed ova** in artificial beds. These have been improved, and can now be supplied capable of hatching 15,000 ova—**Price 22s. 6d. each.** (For full information see chapter on "Hatching the Eggs," in "An Angler's Paradise," 7s. 10d. post free.

Selected Ova can be supplied for these beds at above prices, or from three-year-old Trout in **15,000 lots,** at **£4. 2s. per lot.**

OVA AND FRY PER 1,000.

SALMONIDÆ.

	EYED OVA.			FRY.		
	Per 1,000.			Per 1,000		
	£	s.	d.	£	s.	d.
* Trout (Salmo fario) good mixed breeds ..	0	10	0	1	0	0
* Do. do. carefully selected ...	0	15	0	1	5	0
* Anglo-Swiss Trout (Salmo fario). A magnificent breed (grows very large)	1	0	0	1	10	0
* Kennett Trout (Salmo fario)	1	0	0	1	0	0
* Buttermere Trout (Salmo fario) ... ... *This fish has been crossed with other good breeds, and very materially improved.*	1	0	0	1	10	0
* Loch Kindar Trout (Salmo fario). A splendid fish supposed to have been originally brought from Loch Leven by monks. It has been much improved by cultivation ...	1	0	0	1	10	0

OVA AND FRY.—CONTINUED.

	EYED OVA. Per 1,000.			FRY. Per 1,000		
	£	s.	d.	£	s.	d.
* Loch Leven Trout, good average	0	10	0	1	0	0
* Do. Do. from selected fish ...	0	15	0	1	5	0
* Do. Do. very fine	1	0	0	1	10	0
* Levenensis x fario Hybrids. Recommended	0	10	0	1	0	0
* Fario x Levenensis do. Recommended	0	10	0	1	0	0
Very good crosses made by special request, and for which a demand is growing.						
* Trutta Levenensis Hybrids. An excellent cross between Levens and Sea Trout, that will mature in fresh water	1	0	0	1	10	0
* Rainbow Trout (Salmo irideus), selected ...	1	0	0	2	0	0
* American Trout (Salmo fontinalis), selected ...	0	10	0	1	0	0
* Do. from smaller fish	0	8	0	1	0	0
* Do. the original Troutdale strain, first acclimatised by me in 1869, and then sold at £100 per 1000 ...	1	0	0	1	10	0
* Salmon (Salmo salar)	1	10	0	2	0	0
Do. in lots of 5,000 and up, direct from the hatcheries abroad	1	0	0†		—	
* Sea trout (Salmo trutta)	1	10	0	2	0	0
Do. in lots of 5,000, from abroad ...	1	0	0†		—	
* Sewen (Salmo Cambricus)	2	10	0	3	10	0
* Do. in lots of 5,000 and up	2	0	0	3	0	0
* Great Lake Trout (Salmo ferox)	1	0	0	2	0	0
Do. do. in lots of 5,000 and up ...	0	15	0	1	10	0
* Red Char (Salmo umbla), finest selected ...	3	0	0	3	10	0
* Alpine Char (Salmo Alpinus), finest selected	2	10	0	3	0	0
* Welsh Char (Salmo salvelinus)	2	0	0	2	10	0
* Do. from smaller fish	1	10	0	2	10	0
Char (Alpinus or salvelinus), in lots of 5,000 and up, from abroad	1	5	0†		—	
* Grayling (Salmo thymallus)	2	0	0	3	0	0
* Land-locked Sea Trout (Salmo trutta), from fish bred at the Solway Fishery, and that have never been to sea, but have been thoroughly naturalised to fresh water. A very limited number	2	0	0	3	0	0
* Mixed or remnants	0	8	0	1	0	0

Each season sundry odd lots of ova are taken, as well as experimental lots, and a few hybrids. These are recommended for beginners, or for stocking small ponds where a variety is desired, and are very good value, consisting of Char, Trout, Levens, &c.

*(Ova marked * delivered, carriage paid, to any Railway Station in Britain, or sent free by post at our option. Carriage paid except†).*

Special arrangements have been made for the direct importation of American and Canadian ova of various kinds of Salmonidæ, White Fish, &c. Orders for these should be booked at once.

also as yearling and two-year-old fish, is an eye-opener because Mr Armistead was certainly a believer in widening his interest. There were trout (sea, brown and rainbow), and what he called 'American brook trout', of which he was very proud, having been the first to introduce this fish to England and acclimatize it to English conditions. In 1869 he was selling eyed ova of his American brook trout – 'the original Troutdale strain' – at £100 per thousand, and twenty years later the price had tumbled to £1 per thousand.

Armistead, however, had made a natural error in assuming that the American brook trout was indeed a member of the *Salmo* family (after all it did have spots like those of the trout), and did not know that in fact he was bringing 'coals to Newcastle' because his American brook trout were nothing more than one of an infinite number of varieties of char . . . and the Lakes certainly had enough of those.

Other exotic fish introduced by Armistead included the American black bass and 'German' trout, and he also sold Anglo-Swiss trout (presumably a hybrid he had developed); Kennett, Buttermere, Loch Kindar and Loch Leven trout and a number of hybrids of these 'varieties'; Great Lake trout; red char, Alpine char, Welsh char, grayling, and what he called 'land-locked' sea trout which he had bred himself, which had never been to sea "but had been thoroughly naturalized to fresh water". Study of the natural history of the trout had not yet progressed far enough to reveal that a sea trout is merely a brown trout which has been to sea!

Thousands of the fish raised at Troutdale were introduced into waters all over the country, apparently without upsetting Nature's balance.

By 1870 Armistead had relinquished his hold on the Troutdale hatchery and concentrated all his efforts on his New Abbey project – which is still in being.[2] Now Dr Parnaby was the owner of the Troutdale business and there are several newspaper references to his activities. In 1875 he presented to John Crozier, long-time Master of the Blencathra Foxhounds, "a number of graylings and German trout which have been put into the St. John's and neighbouring rivers about Threlkeld. It is hoped", the report continued, "that anglers will allow them to propagate, and if any are taken at present to return them to the waters."[3]

Then Parnaby started to tackle the local puzzle as to why salmon were never (at that time) found in the Borrowdale reaches of the Derwent, and the universal puzzle regarding the migrating habits of the salmon. Borrowdale folk had for a long time wondered why the salmon never came through Derwentwater to grant them the bounty this rich river granted to other people on its banks. Parnaby decided to take a hand in the matter. "It is said that salmon always return to the river of their birth," he said, "so if I hatch salmon out at my Troutdale hatchery and put them into the river in Borrowdale, they will return, and we will have salmon in Derwentwater and in the Borrowdale Derwent."

He obtained some Derwent salmon in spawning condition and stripped the females of their eggs and the males of their milt, and put the orange-coloured fertilized eggs into his hatching trays at Troutdale. The glass rods of the hatching trays were spaced close enough to hold the eggs, yet wide enough apart to allow the alevins, when they hatched, to fall through to the gravel bed below.

Six weeks after hatching the alevins were run off into the larger rearing tanks where they were fed on grated boiled liver "and other suitable food" until they were about an inch long, and then they were put into the outdoor rearing ponds which were large oblong ponds with gravel bottoms, the sides being of mountain slate, with four or five feet depth of water running through.

In six months the fry were three or four inches long and were under constant supervision from the hatchery attendant, Tom Jenkins, who had his living quarters attached to the hatchery. This was a trying time at the hatchery, and for the people of Borrowdale, because uninvited visitors were often seen off the premises by Jenkins brandishing an axe, or by Parnaby with a shotgun.

Parnaby kept his salmon fry until they had reached the yearling stage, and when they had assumed the bright silver livery of the smolt they were all, thousands of them, marked with little labels attached to the 'dead' adipose fin situated just above the tail.

That done, Parnaby decided to put all his eggs into one basket – or all his fish into one river – and let the lot go in the Derwent above Derwentwater, most of them in the Troutdale stream.

Those which survived predators such as pike and other 'cannibal' fish and managed to run the gauntlet of otters, cormorants, herons and seagulls and the pollution from lead mines in the hills and the coal mines of the lower Derwent Valley, made it to the sea at Workington as 'whiting' (a local Derwent name), 'yellow fins' or 'smolts'.

What happened to salmon after that nobody knew at the time; the secret of the feeding grounds off Greenland was to be safe for most of the next century. All Parnaby could do now was wait, and get on with the normal business of the hatchery.

In the autumn of 1874, a year after the young salmon had been put into the Troutdale back, Tom Jenkins was crossing the beck on a plank bridge which spanned it below the Borrowdale Hotel. He habitually looked into river and beck water for signs of fish, but this time he saw something that took his breath away: a fine grilse, a young salmon fresh up from the sea. He looked closer and on the 'dead' fin on its back saw the tab which had been fixed on the salmon released the previous year.

Tom ran swiftly to the hotel, where he knew he would find Parnaby and, breathlessly, said, "Doctor; theer yan o' them cum back."

"What", asked the Doctor, "are you talking about?"

"Whey, yan o' them young salmon we marked hes cum back."

If Parnaby had been drinking out of the Holy Grail he would have left it on the table as he did a half-finished whisky, and he hurried with Tom to the plank bridge.

And there it was: a salmon which had come through Derwentwater; a salmon which he had reared; a salmon which had, as he had said it would, returned to the river of its birth.

He told Jenkins to get some wire netting to erect a barrier across the beck below the fish to prevent it escaping. The fish was then driven into one of the hatchery ponds where it remained until Parnaby had a special tank constructed for it.

Having proved what had been long suspected about salmon returning to the river of their birth – although this was only one out of several thousand released – the logical thing for Parnaby to have done would be to follow up the experiment by allowing the salmon to breed with eggs or milt (it was never recorded whether it was a male or a female fish) from other parts of the Derwent.

But Parnaby had had so many arguments with other 'experts' about the natural history of the salmon that he just had to keep the salmon as proof of his own particular theories. The fish was sent away in its large glass tank to be put on show at the Fisheries Exhibition in South Kensington.

The salmon was ten pounds in weight. It was the sole survivor of the Troutdale experiment, but there is no record of it having survived its notoriety for long. The salmon cannot be kept in captivity, and the fruit of the Parnaby experiment was sacrificed to the doctor's conceit because, above all things, he had to be able to tell the world what had been achieved, and to produce proof that salmon did in fact return to the rivers of their birth. All it did, of course, was show that this particular salmon had returned to the river of its birth, and Parnaby's experiment aroused some cynicism on the part of men interested in fisheries.

Of course the salmon died in capitivity, and it spent a great deal of time 'on tour' around various committees and scientific societies, stuffed, with the Troutdale tag still attached.

Parnaby's experiment might have turned the upper Derwent into a salmon river and Derwentwater into a salmon-holding lake, but this was extremely unlikely owing to the unpredictability of the 'flash' floods of that stretch of water.

In 1883 the new owners of the Troutdale hatchery (Parnaby had now disappeared from the scene) suggested a new venture in salmon raising. The salmon population of the lower Derwent had been falling rapidly owing to over-fishing, pollution and disease, and the depredations of innumerable poachers along Derwent, Cocker and Marron.

Realizing at last that the Atlantic salmon had no intention of ever using Derwentwater as a holding lake, William Fletcher, then chairman of the Derwent Fishery Board, supported a suggestion from the Troutdale hatchery that an experiment should be tried with 'land-locked' salmon, the *Salmo vernernensis* of Lake Vernern in Switzerland, which hatched in feeder streams and grew to maturity in the lake without ever entering the sea.

The hatchery owners had agreed to lease the hatchery, a number of local anglers supported the scheme, and co-operation was promised from a most unlikely source, Professor Schmidt, Royal Commissioner for Sweden, who had offered 20,000 ova from Lake Vernern as a gift for the experiment. The scheme caught the attention of Professor Huxley, a leading authority, who promised co-operation, but the matter fell through due to apathy, and in some cases strenuous opposition on the part of riparian owners.

Troutdale was claimed as the first 'commercial' fish hatchery in the world, and Armistead later claimed his Solway Fisheries at New Abbey to be the most successful fish hatchery in the world. The strange thing about both Armistead's and Parnaby's salmon operations was that, apart from Parnaby's single experiment, both used, exclusively, eggs imported from abroad, mostly America, and one of Parnaby's more spectacular deals concerned a consignment of American salmon.

The *West Cumberland Times* in 1875 reported that a Mr McAllister, probably a relic of the 'Auld Allience' because his address was La Mauvoisinniere per Ancenia, Loire, Inferieure, had ordered 500 salmon fry from Troutdale.

By any standards the execution of that order was a model. The salmon eggs were sent to Parnaby at Troutdalc by his agent in New Jersey, U.S.A., and hatched in the Troutdale tanks. They were kept a few weeks and then placed in a large glass carboy which was three parts filled with water and placed in a basket in which it was despatched to France on 14 April, arriving at its destination on the 17th.

Having been placed in the carboy the night before despatch, the fry were without a change of water – and without any means of oxygenation either (although the value of oxygenating plants had already been realized) – for nearly ninety hours, and not one of the 500 fry was dead on arrival.

The Troutdale hatchery died slowly. Nothing is heard of operations there after 1883 when its owners offered to lease it for the 'landlocked' salmon experiment. The buildings fell into disrepair; a flash flood in Troutdale breached the dam which deflected the stream through the tanks and almost filled the rearing tanks with gravel.

Eventually the tarred-timber building which covered the hatchery was dismantled, and Nature set to work to erase the scar which the old hatchery left on the placid face of the valley.

Today Troutdale is known to Boy Scouts who camp there, and to a few walkers and climbers, but there is nothing there to interest the angler; nothing in the insignificant trickle of summer water; nothing either in the vestiges of the long, narrow tanks; nothing to indicate that it was here that a little bit of history was made on several occasions, the most significant being the salmon experiment.

Really, Troutdale did not leave any mark on history at all because most of the history books seem to have got it wrong, and have given the credit for the first successful hatching of salmon ova and the first 'homing' salmon to Trout*beck*. This is not an original error in Cumbriana because there used to be regular storms of protest in local and national newspapers about a version of the song 'D'ye ken John Peel?' which averred that he "lived in Trout *beck* once on a day."

Troutdale today, which has a high place in the beauty stakes of Lakeland, seems content in its quiet; happy that those exciting days of experiment are over, and that the great ugly hatchery building is gone. It is not surprising that very few people today know the original purpose of those long, rectangular, slate-lined holes in the ground beside the beck.

8

A Female of the Species

The world of the dalesmen was small in that they were concerned only with that part of the world which they could see from their cottages, and nothing beyond that mattered very much.

A Loweswater lad on his first day at Mary Mirehouse's school on Mockerkin How looked westward over the coastal plain beyond which the Solway glistened and the hills of Galloway peered back at him through the faint summer haze, and returned home to tell his parents: "Frae up theer, y' can tell what a big wurrld it is."

The Wilsons of Watendlath, whose connection with Borrowdale's 'hanging valley' could be traced back 400 years before they left it, used to say that the wall at the end of Watendlath was the end of the world.

It was – to them . . . that long, writhing drystone wall which etches in black the outline of the fell tops as seen from the hamlet. That wall is a monument to generations of Wilsons who built and repaired it, keeping to themselves the last available rood of fellside for sheep pasture.

This seeming nonsense of a wall – a nonesense, knowing that Herdwicks seldom stray far from their native heaf – suggests that this could have been the barrier meant to keep the cuckoo in and ensure eternal spring, and that the true 'gowks' of Borrowdale were the Watendlath folk and not the people of Borrowdale proper. The Wilsons never set any claim on the title, and the Borrowdale folk have shown no anxiety to cast off the 'gowk' tag, so there has been no dispute in the matter.

Gilpin's Tour in 1772 took in Watendlath, and he was impressed. "Watenlath [*sic*]," he wrote,

> is that tract of mountainous country which, coming boldly forward, breaks down abruptly from the South upon the vale of Keswick. To those who are accustomed to mountains, perpendicular motions may be amusing, but to those whose ideas are less elevated, they seemed rather peculiar. And yet there is something unmanly in conceiving a difficulty in traversing a path which we were told the women of the country would ascend on horseback, with their panniers of eggs and butter, and return in the night.

Of the Watendlath scenery, Gilpin wrote that

> for beauty and grandeur [it] was equal, if not superior to anything we had yet seen. Here we found a small lake, about two miles in circumference, through which flows the Lodore. The accompaniments of the river, from the lake of Watenlath to its fall, make the scenery . . . It is a valley so contracted that it affords room for little more than the river and a path at the bottom; while the mountains on each side are so perpendicular that their summits are scarce more asunder than their bases. Many mountains we had seen hanging over the sides of the valley, but to be immured for almost the space of three miles within a chasm of rifted rocks, was a novel circumstance.

Like most of the early visitors, Gilpin was exaggerating, but thanks are due for his description and for his introduction of the women of the valley, for the female of the Watendlath species comes prominently into this chapter.

Today the scramble down the side of the Lodore beck is a worthwhile exercise whether the famed falls are in tame or turbulent mood. The beck falls from pool to pool in a whole scale of water music, one of the deeper notes coming from the Devil's Punchbowl, a great circular hole worn in the bedrock of the stream by cobbles whirled round and round by the force of the current. The cobbles wore the rock, the rock wore down the cobbles, and some of the marble-sized pebbles in the bowl at present probably started off football sized many years ago.

The footsloggers' exit from Watendlath is usually over the pass to Rosthwaite, the hamlet gradually diminishing to toy size, dwarfed by the huge spread of fell above it which is streaked by the old packhorse route to Armboth and

Wythburn still kept visible by the tramp of ramblers' boots.

For a driver, the road to Watendlath is a nightmare; for everybody else it is a delight, especially the signpost which tantalisingly points out the 'permissive' footpath to Lodore, and is becoming as popular a subject for the tourist's camera as Ashness Bridge.

Watendlath, apart from being a self-contained community, was once an important staging point on a busy traffic route, for it was through here that the Borrowdale wool was carried from the monks' grange to Furness, and it was still important after the dissolution of the monastery because the picturesque little packhorse bridge is no earlier than the seventeenth century.

Despite a newly provided car park, Watendlath tries not to be 'touristy'. There was a time when this was a real danger. When Hugh Walpole was a popular author he made Watendlath the home of his heroine Judith Paris, and when his *Vanessa* was made into a film by Hollywood (with Clark Gable as Rogue Herries) there was a danger that Judith Paris might do to Watendlath what Lorna Doone did to Exmoor – or Uncle Tom Cobley to Widecombe-in-the-Moor.

Watendlath and its new owners, the National Trust, shrugged off the Walpole glamour which is now confined to a discreet notice which states that it was at John Greenhouse Farm that Walpole wrote part of his book.

Watendlath needed no fictional heroine. It had one of real flesh and blood, and of some strength of character in the mould of those splendid women Gilpin saw ascending the pass on horseback with their panniers of butter and eggs.

About 1765 there were eight or nine little houses at Watendlath in addition to the three farms which still exist, and there was a wayside tavern beside the little bridge. All the buildings except John Greenhouse, Watendlath Farm and Caffle House have now gone.

Mally Messenger, Watendlath's heroine, was born in one of the smaller houses. She was not a Wilson of 'statesman' stock, but the people of the hamlet were like one family, interdependent one upon the other. They all lived on barley bread baked in a vast iron pan with an iron lid. The pan was placed on a fire of glowing peat, the bread was put inside and more burning peat was heaped on the lid until the bread was cooked. Most communities owned such an 'oven', but Watendlath was different in that its bread was baked in the iron pan while other communities used the 'brick yubben' for bread-baking. Watendlath also had a communal 'brick yubben' but that was reserved for special things like 'geus' (goose) pies and 'stannin' pies for Christmas.

Born at Watendlath, Mally Messenger was reared strong and straight, the strength and straight back coming of constant work and the daily trudge over the pass to a 'dame' school at Rosthwaite.

Education was important to the hinds as well as to the 'statesmen' families. The pride of the statesmen rubbed off on their servant men and women whose family lines ran as far back as their masters', and their lives were full of longings which sent their daughters as well as their sons to some education in order to 'better themselves', or to prepare them for the inevitable emigration to the more lucrative living of the towns.

Mally Messenger was still a Watendlath girl when she won a small measure of fame at 'Squire' Pocklington's great regatta and sports at Derwentwater on 6 September 1782.

Of Joseph Pocklington's regattas, this was the greatest, staged on a Homeric scale. One incident was a battle between the Derwentwater fleet and Derwent Isle which had been fortified and was defended by batteries of guns. "The great amphitheatre of lofty mountains surrounding Keswick's matchless vale will bear a noble part in this tremendous uproar," Pocklington promised in his advertisement in the *Cumberland Pacquet*.

He had chosen for himself the role of commander of the island's defences, prominent among which was the 'Half Moon Battery', a name borrowed from Whitehaven, whose Half Moon Battery had succumbed only four years previously to a boatload of John Paul Jones's sailors without firing a single shot. Perhaps Pocklington was having a sly dig at the naval authorities in his choice of names, and his intention of defending the island *successfully*, but it misfired, and the Navy – which owned the old Derwentwater estates through the Royal Naval Hospital at Greenwich – refused him the use of Crow park for his regatta sports in subsequent years.[1]

The regatta and battle went off without a hitch. The surrounding fells played their 'noble' part in echoing and re-echoing the roar of the cannon as they filled the air with noise, smoke and showers of sphagnum moss which, somebody had discovered, made excellent wadding for the gun charges.

The boatmen rowed their boats in a race, and the 'fair ones' raced for a holland smock. Purdy of Whitehaven won the boat race; Mally Messenger won the holland smock.

> Her eager face and streaming hair came rushing in the van, and her bare, shapely legs twinkled past the winning post, and she stood, panting and flushed, with sparkling eyes and ruddy, plump arms flashing above her comely neck, and with trembling hands gathered up her bright locks above her triumphant brows, whilst Derwentwater shone glorious as if participating in her success, and the united voices of the whole parish cheered, and the very mountains seemed to clasp their hands. What victor ever had a fuller triumph, and what rapture could be greater than swelled in Mally's panting bosom?

The words are those of David Lietch who didn't see the race, but pictured it seventy years later to set the scene for another act in Mally Messenger's life.

Mally won the race every time it was held, and as long as they lived her friends remembered her striking, athletic figure. She outlived all her contemporaries, keeping fit and disparaging the trend of 'gentility' among women of the time; assuming an authoritative manner which was discouraging for her many suitors, for though she was often courted she never wed.

At one stage in her life, as women tended always to do until comparatively recent times, she called a halt to changes in her mode of dress in the name of 'fashion'. At that time the 'shoulder brat' was being worn, and the shoulder brat Mally Messenger wore until the day she died. It seems to have been a sort of apron worn from the shoulder, either like a plaid, or neck-high and held with shoulder straps.

She was a restless creature and longed to see the world, and so she travelled to the world's centre, London, and she travelled on foot. Several times she went there, and once, fancying a small stand table she saw in a shop, she bought it and carried it home on her shoulder.

Mostly she walked alone because there were few men who could keep pace with the long, loping stride of the fellman which Mally had kept from her fellside childhood. Once, on her way home, she was passed by a Keswick man, riding horseback. "Good day, Mally," he said, "I'll tell them in Keswick that you're coming."

That was at Ambleside, but Mally was the more determined traveller, and passing the welcoming signs of the Red Lion at Grasmere, the Swan at Dunmail Raise, the Nag's Head at Wythburn, and the King's Head at Thirlspot, she beat her friend into Keswick by some hours, and was fond of telling people about it for years afterwards.

Time moved on for Mally Messenger. Her early education was now paying a dividend because she was running a small 'dame' school, and now the only person alive who wore the old fashioned 'shoulder brat' which had been out of fashion for half a century.

Dr Lietch encountered her "still hale and heart-whole at ninety", teaching a small boy to read:

> This ancient sybil bending her thin frame and brown antique features, and unspectacled eyes, on the Sacred Book, on the well worn page of which lay her withered hand; her skinny fingers creeping, like Time, slowly along the lines and down the page; her voice, like Tradition, dropping fragments of lore on the bewildered young learner, who was a small, blank-eyed, soft-cheeked, rosy youngster, fumbling hard at some marbles or other like treasures in his pocket with one hand, while the other followed the fingers of Mally over the page – a most strange and touching spectacle.
>
> The faithful earnestness and painful energy of the ancient teacher; the enforced attention and slow industry of the child; the young and old fingers on the sacred page; both Mally's hands and all her thoughts engaged with the book; one of the child's hands and half his thoughts busy with his secret treasures; the

row of little boys and girls seated idly in various positions on the opposite form, whom a glance out of the corner of the old schoolmistress's eye kept in tolerable quiet – there was something very touching and unwonted in the whole scene, wonder at her age and faculties, and over all lay the feeling of respect for the honourable industry which could thus induce the old woman to maintain her independence, and still act a useful part, so long after the day's work of man and woman are done.

Mally Messenger was an example of the independence, and of the superior energy and longevity, of the dalesfolk. She was liked and respected by all who knew her, and known to everybody as 'Mally'. It was only at her death in 1856 that the local newspaper gave her real name: Mary.

As the *Derwentwater Record* said when announcing her passing to a sorrowing town and district: "Mally Messenger, if not one of the celebrities of the place, was at least one of the notabilities of Keswick."

9

Images in Rock and Fell

Seeing pictures in the fire was a popular pastime in pre-television, pre-central-heating days, a pastime which gave full rein to childish imagination because the fire in the hearth is never the same in any two seconds, and has a special magic because no two people ever see the same picture.

There is no comparison, one would think, between pictures in an ever-changing fire and images seen in the fells, the great unchanged, unchanging faces of Lakeland.

But the scene of fell and lake is always changing in mist, haze and clear air; in rain, cloud and clear sky. The seasons change the colours, and even 'dead' colours can change as the bracken proves when it turns a deeper russet after a shower. As autumn brings in its train a feast of colour in woodlands and on the fellside, so the shining of the sun when the year is still young brings the lichen on dry-stone walls into luminous life. This is the magic the Lake Country shares with the pictures in the fire: what you see in any moment of time nobody has ever seen before, and nobody will ever see again.

There are, of course, images which everybody can see who has eyes to see and which are as unchanging at St Paul's Cathedral.

There is one Lakeland 'curiosity' which changes as you pass it. Helm Crag has been called 'The Lion and the Lamb' by generations of conductors of eight-lakes tours because, approaching from Keswick, the summit crags take the form of a crouching lion about to eat some less recognizable thing and which was turned into 'lamb' probably, but unconsciously, for alliteration's sake.

From different angles the Lion and the Lamb turn into a witch, into a man sitting at a grand piano with the lid up. Further along the road and the man still sits at the piano which has turned miraculously into an upright.

Strangely enough, there are people who see nothing of this in the rocks which crown Helm Crag, but they probably wouldn't see pictures in the fire either.

Out of the darkness of Stoke Poges churchyard Thomas Gray conjured some of the most wonderful imagery in English literature for his *Elegy*, but the Lion and Lamb escaped him, for on passing Dunmail Raise he saw Helm Crag only "Like a gigantic building demolished". West, author of *The Antiquities of Furness*, called it "a mass of antedeluvian ruins". In his notes to 'The Waggoner' Wordsworth called Helm Crag "a mountain of Grasmere, the broken summit of which represents two figures, full as distinctly shaped as that of the famous Cobbler near Arroquhar in Scotland", and with Benjamin his Waggoner traversing the Raise in dull, leaden weather sees

> . . . a lurid light,
> Above Helm Crag – a streak half dead,
> A burning of portentous red;
> And near that lurid light, full well
> The ASTROLOGER, sage Sidrophel,
> Where at his desk and book he sits,
>   Puzzling aloft his curious wits;
> He whose domain is held in common
> With no one but the ANCIENT WOMAN,
> Cowering beside her rifted cell,
> As if intent on magic spell; –
>   Dread pair that, in spite of wind and weather,
> Still sit upon Helm-crag together!

Wordsworth cannot be accused here of lacking imagination, even if this passage is not one of the better parts of 'The Waggoner' and reminds one of the poorer passages in Scott's 'Lay of the Last Minstrel'.

The Cumbrian poet did see other strange sights, but had perfectly logical explanations for them. There was the day when he saw a magnificent castle reflected in the still surface of Ullswater, but this, he knew, was Lyulph's Tower, that extravagant summer house of the old Dukes of Norfolk, which was invisible directly because of a bank of mist. Again, a freak of lighting once showed him an extra island in his beloved Grasmere which he later explained as a reflection, from a bed of ice which had been thinly covered by water, of the fell Silver How behind.

From West Cumberland the outline of the Whiteside and Hobcarton tops appear as the outline of a recumbent effigy of a man which had the old weavers of lore claiming it as the effigy of a long-dead and unnamed king . . . about three miles long!

A more famous illusion is the Castle Rock of Triermain in the Vale of St John, but down-to-earth dalesmen never saw it as anything but Green Crag, its old name, although slight traces of fortification on its top suggest that the 'Castle' part of its name could have a meaning stretching much farther back than Sir Walter Scott's celebrated romance or William Hutchinson's fanciful description.

Southey, never a man to be accused, in the vernacular, of 'seeing things', did, however, see a sight "both dreamy and wonderful" which was a perfect reflection in mirror-smooth Derwentwater of the Catbells range.

There must, however, be something in the air of that district which Southey loved so well, for it was here that he dreamed up that wonderful story for the little folk, 'The Story of the Three Bears'. Here also, according to the local tradition, the young Beatrix Potter, on holiday, first encountered Peter Rabbit in the garden of Fawe Park. And for good measure, another regular and welcome inhabitant of the district, Molly Lefebure, invented 'Scratch and Co.' stories which, like Southey's 'Three Bears', are read with interest by both children and adults.

The imagery of the 'lakers' really knows no bounds, and in no field does imagination run madder riot than in rock climbing.

Napes Needle can be excused for it is what a rock-hound accepts as 'needle-shaped', but still it is a name which catches the imagination to such effect that once there was a belief that rock climbers could perform a manoeuvre called 'threading the needle', but this writer never saw it being done or even ever heard of it being done.

Among the crags on Gable's Napes is the well-known Sphinx Rock which is more than an optical illusion because the great Red Indian Chief profile has provided the foreground for innumerable photographs of Wasdale Head's intricate pattern of walls.

The naming of rock climbs seems to have depended on the erudition and particular interests of the god-parents, so that Greek and Latin names crop up which did not tax greatly the ingenuity of anybody who had put in some time in the lower forms of a moderate school.

Many of the names range from the cynical – who but a cynic could have named Pillar's 'Appian Way'? – to the outright humorous, for only a humorist could have named 'Amen Corner' on Dow Crag. Considering the sort of language which has issued from this notoriously strenuous and awkward pitch, 'Amen' seems the most inapt name which could have been chosen.

There are other names which indicate that the early climbers were not averse to grasping at straws. There is a Tennis Court ledge on Scawfell's Moss Ghyll, which is hardly big enough for tiddlywinks, and an Oval on that same crag's magnificent Central Buttress on which it would be impossible to organize a game of marbles, but one supposes that the names are intended to suggest how their discoverers felt about them when they got there. It is a fact attested by almost everybody who has climbed Central Buttress that the Oval seems the size of a cricket pitch once you have left it to strive with the infamous Flake Crack.

And Collie's Step in Moss Ghyll, the cutting of which nearly created a furore in the days of 'purist' rock-climbing as being an 'artificial aid', was little more than a scratch on the rock, the term 'step' being somewhat misleading to timid tyros in days gone by.

But there is a mantelshelf on Napes Needle hardly big

enough to hold a brass candlestick, and a Buttonhook at Kern Knotts; a Sepulchre even because it is a graveyard of hopes of many who thought to climb it.

Least imaginative of all names of Lakeland 'attractions' is Bowder Stone' which is merely what it says – 'Boulder Stone'. Some visitors and writers have likened this immense piece of rock to a stranded or unlaunched ship, which was probably apposite when ships were chunkier than they are today. The Bowder still has its attractions; still draws a large number of visitors who do not today have the benefit of the wisdom of a one-time custodian of the Stone who, when asked how it got there, replied, with uncustomary reverence because he was noted for his rich vocabulary: "God put it there."

Bowder Stone is indeed a work of Nature in that it was deposited where it is probably by a dying glacier, but it required the art of man to complete the picture and 'Squire' Pocklington of the famous Derwentwater regattas is credited with giving impetus to the excavation of the ground around the Bowder to emphasize its extraordinary balance.[1]

Another work of Nature, assisted to some extent by man, is the 'Bishop of Barf', that whitened obelisk of rock which sticks out like a new-bandaged sore thumb above the Swan Hotel at Thornthwaite. Its first known name was The Monk, and it was well enough known for people to wish to see it. However, it required an ascent of the fellside to get a proper view of it, and the Thornthwaite folk, probably tired of trying to point it out to visitors, or of guiding them up the fellside to see it, had it whitewashed. It was then promoted and became The Abbott. Later it became a Bishop and the legend of the Bishop of Barf was born – that once upon a time there was a Bishop who was killed when trying to win a bet by riding his horse up (or down) the fellside.

The Bishop is whitewashed at fairly regular intervals, the going rate for the job at the time of writing being a quart of ale according to a veritable stream of television reporters who have gone there about The Bishop for 'Tonight', 'Look North', 'Nationwide', *et al.*

The Bishop (or Monk, or Abbott) provided entertainment

for the locals of the parish of Thornthwaite, as the 'gowk' stories did for the people of Borrowdale, and Will Ritson's 'greet lees' for the people of Wasdale, at a time when the Swan stood at the end of a road because the road which now connects it with the Pheasant at the other end of Bassenthwaite Lake shore is, comparatively speaking, 'new'.

Mention of the Pheasant at Peil Wyke brings to mind another Lakeland illusion which has nothing at all to do with fell or lake, mist, fog or frost. Peil Wyke is the spot where, according to legend, the last fairy in Cumberland was seen.

The story goes that a man was climbing Castle How at Peil Wyke[2] when he stumbled at one of the defensive walls of this Celtic hill fort and overturned a boulder. When he turned round there was a little man in a green suit sitting on the boulder. He turned away, then looked again and the little man had gone.

The fact that the man had emerged to climb the hill from the Pheasant, which long had a reputation for the best home-brew in the district, could have had something to do with this last sighting of one of the 'little people'. But this extremely questionable sighting had nothing at all to do with the name which as been given to the flat top of Castle How, Peil Wyke – The Fairy Glen. That, it seems, is a name which has grown spontaneously about the place. There must be something in the air!

In connection with the sighting of the last fairy in Cumberland, it is worth noting also that 'monsters' have been sighted in Bassenthwaite Lake!

10

"A Plaister Taken Inwardly

There is no statistical proof that the average Cumbrian is bigger than the average Northumbrian, Lancastrian, Yorkshireman or man of Kent. The popular picture of the tall dalesman, descended direct from Norse stock, long of limb and heavy of body, is one which persists, however.

The truth is that there are as many small people as there are big people because the Cumbrian today is a veritable cocktail of the British races due to immigration of off-comers to live in comfort, or to work hard in the industries of the west coast and the Carlisle plain.

It is, however, true that Cumbria has proved a fruitful recruiting ground for the various regiments of Guards – and particularly the Scots Guards – and the Metropolian Police, all of whom require recruits of taller-than-average stature.

There is a noticeable difference between the average dalesman and the average townsman of Cumbria. Indigenous dalesmen and their close relatives are usually taller than the men of Workington or Whitehaven. The difference is probably due to the healthy life lived by the dalesmen and their forebears in comparison with the conditions of life in a district sweating in the throes of the Industrial Revolution and subject to the many illnesses endemic in heavily industrialized and distinctly unhygienic areas.

One advantage the dalesman had over his cousin employed in industry: he was seldom, if ever, short of food.

He was fortunate in that he was easily satisfied, and though he lived on a diet which would make the compilers of modern Good Food Guides retch, it was a diet which was both satisfying and sustaining. 'Plain' and 'homely' are words which have been used to describe the diet, and the reader of modern writers on Lakeland would expect these words to cover such vernacular dishes as 'tatie pot' and 'barley bannocks', with delights like rum butter and stannin' pie ennobling the fare at feast times.[1]

In fact the diet of Cumbrians 'lang sen' was much humbler than that. That near-forgotten cereal crop, the oat, was its basis, and the form in which it was eaten was porridge, or, in the vernacular, 'poddish'.

Starting in the realm of folklore, the 'Cork Lad of Kentmere' ate porridge. How he came to be called the Cork Lad of Kentmere is a problem, unless it was because Cumbrian traditions insist upon spotlighting its more colourful characters with 'by-neams' or 'nick-names'.

One version of the story says his name was Gilpin, another that he was called Hugh Herd, but both are obviously the same man because the exploits in which he engaged are common to both stories. Confusion about his name is understandable because, according to tradition, his mother was a nun of Furness who had been driven out on to the world at the Dissolution. She bore her son and she lived by begging from house to house being fortunate, in the end, in finding a house at Troutbeck which was of such small value that its existence was almost forgotten, and the woman and her son lived peaceably there until it was granted to a local landlord who went to take possession of it.

The lad, disliking the thought of his mother losing her home, and having now grown up, threw the new owner out on his ear. This unheard-of liberty reached official ears and the lad had to go to London to plead his case. At London he found that the popular spectator sport of the time was wrestling. He watched with some interest, but was unimpressed, especially by the King's champion who had thrown all his opponents. The lad mounted the platform to try a fall with the champion and threw him with ease.

Displeased, the champion claimed that it was not a fair fall, so they 'took hod' again, and with a crushing bear-hug the lad broke his opponent's back, threw him off the platform and asked the referees if they thought *that* was a fair fall.

The King sent for the lad and asked him his name and where he came from, and he replied that he did not know his own name, but said, "Folk commonly call me the Cork Lad of Kentmere."

When the King asked him what he lived on, he replied, "Thick porridge, that a mouse might walk on dry-shod, to me breakfast; the sunny side of a wedder[2] to my dinner when I can get it."

Wishing to reward the new champion, the King asked him if he had a desire for any particular thing, and the lad said that all he asked for was the home his mother lived in, the paddock behind it to get peat for fuel, and liberty to cut wood for the fire in Troutbeck Park.

These the King granted and the Cork Lad went back to his home to live happily ever after. He used his great strength in the service of the King in Border battles, and in the service of his neighbours in performing such tasks as lifting into position the great chimney beam in the pele tower of Kentmere.

Apparently he took the business of displaying his strength too seriously, for he was enjoying his favourite pastime of pulling trees out by the roots when he suffered a strain and died from it at the age of forty-two.

If the Cork Lad of Kentmere was a good advertisement for the good, healthy living Cumbria offered, he had many followers in generations of great wrestlers who won more than local fame, and quite large numbers of Rugby League forwards, many of whom won international honours.

However, back to 'poddish'.

It was about halfway through the eighteenth century when an off-comer settled in Keswick to take up his profession as a physician. One day he was asked by a visiting colleague how he liked the life at Keswick.

"My situation", he replied, "is a very eligible one as a gentleman; I can enjoy every species of country amusement in the greatest perfection. I can fish, hunt and shoot among a profusion of game of every kind; the neighbouring gentlemen too seem to vie with each other in acts of politeness. But as a physician, I cannot say it is quite so alluring to me, for the natives have got the art of preserving their health and prolonging their lives without boluses or electuaries, by a plaister taken inwardly, called thick porridge. This protects them from the various diseases which shake the human fabric, and makes them slide into the grave without pain by the gradual decays of Nature."

However there were, in 1811, signs of the rot setting in.

Jollie's *Sketch of Cumberland Manners and Customs* speaks of the "homely but wholesome fare, rather peculiar to this county" and goes on to mention barley bread and "hasty pudding, or thick pottage", "a dish which almost universally forms the breakfast, and often the supper: it is made of oatmeal boiled with water to a thick pulp, and is eaten along with a little butter, milk, treacle or beer, according to the taste of the person, or convenience of the family."

To this coarse diet Jollie adds bread and skimmed milk cheese (the famed Whillimoor[3] cheese) but laments that "these simple and healthy supporters of human life, which have swelled the massy bulk and huge limbs of thousands of rustics, and preserved them to a good old age unattacked by the train of diseases attendant on modern luxury, have latterly been a little ousted by tea and butcher's meat."

The rot was indeed setting in because Jollie continued: "tea is not uncommonly the breakfast of the farmer and his wife; and even the wives of mechanics often feel their stomachs too delicate now-a-days for the digestion of hasty pudding and boiled milk." Society was on the downward slide when the "wives of mechanics" – the term 'mechanic' was generally applied to all men in manufacturing industry – had departed from the diet which had supported their ancestors in work and play, especially work, for centuries.

Even the farmers, those stalwart upholders of tradition in almost every sense of the word, were on the downward slide and Jollie commented: "Farmers also at present reserve out of the beef and mutton they sell to the butchers a much larger quantity for the use of their own tables than formerly."

Traditional crops were also on the way out because modern improvements were raising four or five times more wheat than was produced of yore; "Consequently they use it more freely in tea cakes, pies and puddings," wrote Jollie. (The 'tea cake' mentioned here is what today would in other parts of the country be called a 'bread roll' or a 'bap' in its substance, but which was larger than either of these modern products, and in Cumberland was generally called a 'biskey'.

"In short," Jollie concluded, "luxury and refinement are fast creeping in upon the Cumbrians; a change which is seen and generally regretted by the old people, who agree that in consequence thereof, the present rising generation, is a puny race of beings compared with their ancestors."

However, even the despondent Jollie had to admit that all was not yet lost, and in his concluding sentence remarks: "But this alteration is most apparent in the more cultivated [he does not make it clear whether he means 'cultivated' in the agricultural or social sense] parts of the county, and in the vicinity of market towns; in the remote districts and about the skirts of the mountains, these innovations are still kept at bay, or their advances but tardily admitted."

William Dickinson of Workington, in his *Cumberland Farm Life in Old Times*, published in his *Cumbriana* in 1876, leaves no doubt about the farmers' diet "When George the third was king", for,

> Their habit o' leevin was poddish at mworn,
> And taties and point at neunn:[4]
> To let thersels down wi' tea they wad scworn,
> So they poddish't at eebnin' seunn.

Almost exactly a century after Jollie's *Sketch* was published, the Cumbrians' straying from traditional eating habits was once more under scrutiny, and again poddish and the humble oat were put forward almost as the elixir of life.

Never in all its history has there been a more fervent admirer of the Lakes and its people than Canon Rawnsley, Vicar of Crosthwaite. He was always prepared to express an opinion about anything of interest to him or the general public from Home Rule for Ireland to the drawbacks he saw in turning good grass into silage and feeding it to defenceless farm animals. One of the things which aroused his interest and his antipathy was white bread. Whether the Canon or his wife ever indulged themselves with white bread is not known, but white bread for the masses was, according to him, definitely not on; it was ruining the health of the nation. In 1910 Canon Rawnsley gave vent to his feelings about white bread in a letter to the Editor of the *Daily News*. It was a matter of pride in Cumbria and Cumbrians that sparked off his interest. He was disturbed to discover that those of Cumberland's sturdy sons who had offered themselves as recruits to the Metropolitan Police had been found suitable in every way but one. They were physically strong; they had all passed the height test (the 'Met' then had a rule limiting recruiting to men over 5 feet 10 inches tall) and the intelligence test. But when their teeth were examined, every man Jack of them in that year had failed the test.

"Why?" asked Canon Rawnsley, a purely rhetorical question because he had the answer immediately at hand. "There is something radically wrong with the food," he wrote to *The Daily News*, and he added that the root cause was the steel-milling of the flour and the subsequent refining which removed the inner cuticle of the wheat corn which contained the calcium which strengthened the enamel of the teeth. The remedy, he suggested was a return to stone-ground flour, unrefined, which would mean that growing children would not be deprived of "the very instruments that most tend to good nutrition" – their teeth. "My experience of stone-ground flour", wrote the Canon,

> is that the mere fragrance and scent of it – if one becomes accustomed to it – makes it impossible for one to return to the scentless, tasteless flour that is in fashion. I am told that one of the cuticles of wheat grain which is cast out in the new milling process contains certain essential oils which give this nutty fragrance, and that this essential oil has a peculiar power to promote the flow of saliva and therefore is an important aid to digestion.

Again, it is unknown whether or not Canon Rawnsley allowed nothing but stone-ground wholemeal flour at his table, and, if he did insist on it, where he got it, because stone-ground flour was already just a memory in Cumbria. But if it could be got, the Canon, traditionalist to the last, declared that it should be baked into bread only in the traditional way: in brick ovens.

Well, the 'brick yubben' had also had its day by 1910, and there were probably none left in action with the coming of the 'combination' cast-iron, black-leaded and brass-knobbed kitchen grate which was installed in even the humblest of colliers' cottages right down into the lowest strata of society in West Cumberland.[5] No brick ovens! The Canon had an answer even to that apparently insoluble problem. His suggestion was a return to the making of 'haver-bread' – an almost lost art – which dispensed with an oven and used instead a 'girdle', a flat hotplate of iron to bake wafer-thin cakes of oatmeal bread.

It was, wrote Rawnsley, the staple bread of the dales, "the flat brod which came in with the Norse conquerors of Cumberland". Not only was it valuable as a staple food; it was also labour and fuel-saving, because only two bakings took place in a year, and the haver-bread was stored in the old 'kists' or chests, which were part of the furniture of every farmhouse.

What the Canon did not mention was that to dry out haver-bread which might be affected by the damp which pervaded almost all the houses build the 'old' way (i.e. of dry-stone walls without mortar), bread cupboards were built into the thickness of the walls beside the chimney breasts to keep the bread in condition, and that the oatmeal often had to be conditioned in a similar cupboard.

The *Daily News* was a widely-read newspaper, and it and Canon Rawnsley were inundated with letters asking how this super-bread could be made. A week later he gave the *Daily News* readers the recipe and the method. "The iron girdle", he wrote, "is a sheet of iron threequarters of an inch thick, four feet long and two feet broad, which is heated by a small oven fire of coal, or wood and bracken, which, as it is beneath one end of the girdle iron, allows that end to be hotter!"

Oatmeal was mixed with water into a stiff paste, unleavened and unseasoned, lifted out in pieces the size of a cricket ball, and rolled out – in dry oatmeal on a board – into the circular cakes an eighth of an inch thick. The cake was turned on the board and rolled out again so that plenty of dry oatmeal was worked into both surfaces, and then the cake, now approximately eighteen inches in diameter, was put on the hot end of the girdle and baked. It was baked briefly on each side, and then moved to the cooler end of the girdle for drying and crisping.

The work was continuous, and in a day up to six stones of oatmeal could be baked into haver-bread. Well made, and kept in a cool, dry place, haver-bread would keep for six months.

The making of haver-bread varied from place to place, said the Canon, but only in details such as the type of fuel used in the fire, some preferring peat, some wood, and some dry bracken. But the basic ingredient was the same everywhere: stone-ground oats.

Always a super-enthusiast for his particular enthusiasm of the time, Canon Rawnsley also advocated a return to 'poddish', but times were changing and the old, rough, gritty oatmeal was already giving way to Quaker for porridge, and breakfasts and suppers were changing anyway towards more sophisticated foods; and the day was dawning when 'white' was to be the favourite colour of the model housewife, whether it was for the clothes she washed or the bread she baked. Oh yes; she still baked her own bread for no housewife in either urban or rural Cumbria dared, even in those days, be seen going into a shop to *buy* bread.

Two wars have seen the whiteness of our bread fade into the rather greyer shades of less well refined, and probably more nutritious, flour; but the subsequent post-war reaction has always been for a return to white or whiter than that.

Canon Rawnsley's efforts to turn the clock back for our eating habits were unavailing, but today he would find strong support among people who spend small fortunes in 'health-food' shops.

The canny Canon, always with an eye to the domestic economy of the working – and too often workless – classes, believed (and he was probably correct in his belief) that the foods which really promoted good health were those which were cheapest, and in his day there wasn't anything cheaper than oatmeal.

But then oats were the principal grain crop in Cumbria; today it is mostly barley, and one looks almost in vain for a single field of oats in areas where it was literally the staff of life.

To poddish

Canon Rawnsley had some authority behind his claim for poddish as the complete, health-giving food. About 1910 he met an old woman of ninety-three in the street and asked her the secret of her old age. She told him and he put it in a poem which he recited at the next Keswick Old Folks' dinner:

As I came down the Keswick Street
I met a body of ninety-three.
She was straight of back and strong of feet,
And this is what she said to me:
"You ask me why so lish I go,
'Twas poddish, barn, that made me so!

"What, barn, in oor foor-elders' days,
When 'merry-neets' were aw the thing;
When fwoaks greavv'd peat to make a blaze,
An' fiddlers went a-Christmassing;
We grew oor oats, we kept a coo,
An' supped oor poddish aw t'year through.

"Good harden sark oor mothers made,
We carded woo', we larned to spin;
Dressmakkin' was not then the trade,
An' household wark was thowt no sin.
Powsowdies for oor Christmas doo
We hed – but supped oor poddish too.

"We didn't clash oorsels wid tea,
We'd milk an' havver-bread to eat,
And that is why i'm ninety-three
And t' old folks' do is still a treat.
If you would have your old age so,
To poddish back you all must go."[6]

11

A Huddle of Hermits

The Lake District is not the most promising territory for hermits, if only because of the weather. True, hermits, for reasons varying from the holy to the profane, dedicate themselves to a rough life, but even they must draw the line somewhere, and anybody with any sense would, it is supposed, draw that line somewhere south of the southernmost bounds of the Lakes.

Cumbria has, nevertheless, had more than a fair share of people who can qualify for the title of 'hermit', living in different styles from the absolute ascetic of St Herbert of Derwentwater to the near-sybaritic of Millican Dalton who, although he lived in a cave, slept under an eiderdown; from the aesthetic of Fred Leake who was drawn by the incredible beauty of the district and decided to stay, to the eccentric worldliness of the Skiddaw hermit who, from all accounts, was only here, figuratively speaking, for the beer.

Herbert (or Herebert, as Bede calls him) was a lifelong friend of Cuthbert of Lindisfarne but, because of his retiring nature, of less consequence as a historical character. About the middle of the seventh century, Herbert lived an anchorite's life in a little cell he built on the island in Derwentwater which is named after him, a life fashioned on that of Martin of Tours, and of Ninian, the Apostle of the Picts, whose influence was strong in the early Celtic Church.[1]

One of Herbert's claims to fame is that it was his dearest wish that he would die at the same time as Cuthbert, and he got his wish in 688. The hermit died and was buried and his rest has since been undisturbed; the more important Cuthbert rested for nearly two centuries and then, when the Danes invaded, the monks of Lindisfarne took up his coffin and other holy relics and set off on a long journey to prevent Cuthbert's body falling into the hands of the pagans. Eventually the body came to rest in Durham Cathedral, but part of its wanderings was in Cumbria where several churches are dedicated to Cuthbert in remembrance of the fact that his body rested there.

Nobody knows where Herbert is buried. It could be on the island because the little chapel where he received penitents for the confessional was for centuries a place of pilgrimage, whereas the other likely burial place, St Kentigern's Church, Crosthwaite, was not.

It is difficult to wander through the streets of Keswick and remain unaware that once upon a time there was a man who went under the title of 'The Skiddaw Hermit' who frequented the local pubs. It says a lot for the tolerance of Keswick landlords – and remember this is the district where, it was once said, "the hotels are like palaces, and the landlords like princes" – that they let the Skiddaw Hermit in at all; it says much for the turn tourism has taken that one of the more favoured and opulent of the local hostelries should announce on a plaque outside that this was once the resort of, among such illustrious names as Wordsworth, Southey, Tennyson and Shelly, 'The Skiddaw Hermit'.

As 'The Skiddaw Hermit' he has gone down in local history, but Keswickians, with commendable geographical exactitude, called him 'The Dodd Man' because it was actually on Skiddaw Dodd that he lived. His home has been described as a "nest", a "tent of branches", and, more spectacularly, as "a huge, basket-shaped erection of tree branches and bracken which he entered from the top, like a chitty's nest". Anybody who has seen a chitty's (wren's) nest will get the picture.[2] He set up his roost beside a crag and made his bed of bracken and old sacks.

A native of Pitsligo in Aberdeenshire, the Dodd Man came to Keswick as a tramp. The time of his arrival is not definitely known, but he was in his roost on Dodd in the early 1860s, and when he descended into Keswick the inhabitants could hardly ignore him. He wore no coat, hat or shoes, his only attire being a wincey shirt, trousers cut off at the knees, and a beard.

"More like an Irishman than a Scotsman", said one who knew him, because, unlike the dour Scot, the Dodd Man was a great talker, and he talked himself into many drinking schools for free liquor. He was not always a scrounger, sometimes paying his way by selling his own paintings, his speciality being portraits, and he is said to have painted every publican in Keswick, being paid in ale and whisky. At least two of these portraits survive in the possession of a family in Canada. They were painted when the Dodd man was a 'regular' at the Woolpack. He claimed to be able to 'read bumps', but his phrenology was practised more for laughs than anything else and he gave some hilarious performances.

Keswick seems to have liked the Dodd Man who was clean in his habits; at any rate he once washed his single shirt in the nearest beck and let it dry on his back.

But fame, even just a local fame, did the Dodd man little good, because he tended to become unruly when drunk and then he would land in the local lock-up. The patience of the police wore thin, and after a few warnings they had him up before the magistrates. The Dodd Man could not or would not pay the fine, so he was sent to Carlisle Gaol. He returned there repeatedly; even Carlisle Gaol was a nice change from his Skiddaw roost on a winter night.

Eventually the police drove him from his roost, and from Keswick, and he went to Windermere where he lived on the lake shore in a little tent he made himself. For a brief period the holiday trade of Windermere thought that Keswick's loss would be their gain, but the Dodd Man was now overtly violent, and after he had attacked a few visitors, the police escorted him to the parish boundary whence he turned due west and landed at Millom. Millom didn't want him either, so he went to Barrow.

The sad thing about it was that the man had reformed just

before he left Windermere, having been converted by a preacher from Liverpool who conducted services on the lake shore. Eventually he gave up the drink, adopted a more normal mode of attire, and returned to his native Scotland where he died in 1876.

After his departure from Keswick the legend started to grow around the Dodd Man, and to his undoubted skill as a painter and his 'gift' of phrenology was added a wholly unearned reputation for versifying, and at a time when the literary world was trying hard to pretend that John McGonegal did not exist, the following lines were attributed to George Smith, the Skiddaw Hermit:

The lovely sun is setting in the south,
Amongst a throne of silvery clouds,
The placid vale is smiling all round its mouth,
And a ghostlike mist the landscape shrouds.

If he was literate, that sounds like the Dodd Man; he would have altered the path of the sun to find a rhyme, and even McGonegal could not do worse than having the placid vale 'smiling all round its mouth'. But even McGonegal was not capable of the final verse:

A smell comes floating on the ambient air,
Although the fruitful source is hidden;
I cannot see it anywhere,
But think it is the village midden.

If the Dodd Man did write this, and there must be a question over it, because if it is bad, it is eloquently so, it is small wonder that he was driven out of a district which gave birth to Wordsworth and had played host to Southey, Coleridge and company.[3]

It is a thought that the Skiddaw Hermit, barefoot, in wincey shirt and cut-off trousers, would hardly be noticed in Keswick today where eccentricity of garb is normal and eccentric behaviour does not cause the residents to bat an eyelid.

The Dodd Man was hardly a hermit in the true sense of the word, and neither was Barty, a character who infested the

Loweswater Valley for a long time early in the nineteenth century. Who Barty was and where he came from was a matter which exercised the natural curiosity of the dalesfolk, but he gave nobody any satisfaction. The probability is that he was a West Cumbrian, that he was a gipsy with the born name of Barton, and that he had been banished from his tribe. He was given to poaching and stealing, and put pursuers off his trail by tying shoes, back to front, to his feet to give the impression that he had gone the other way. The only mark Barty left is a shallow cave above Scale Hill Wood which is still called 'Barty's Chair'.

Barty had a successor in 'Crutchy', another odd character who also lived occasionally in Barty's Chair. Crutchy was one of the world's unfortunates. Born in Whitehaven, he was both orphaned and crippled as an infant, and he grew up using a single crutch, hence his name. Apprenticed to a tailor, he ran away and joined a mountebank troop selling quack remedies – the origin of the 'Medicine Show' of the Wild West of America – and he left them to join the gipsies who taught him a lot about living off the land.

He left the gipsies and went to Lorton where a sympathetic farmer took him in, clothed and fed him and sent him next day to the Sunday School. He made some progress under John Sorrell, the teacher, but those were the days when abnormalities were jokes, and Crutchy became the butt of his schoolmates. He responded by using his crutch as a weapon, and his tormentors complained. His benefactor sustained his faith in Crutchy for a year but the cripple was accused of thieving and eventually banished. Now fourteen, if he had been abandoned in Lorton parish he would have been a charge on the parish rate, so the farmer put him in his cart and abandoned him in Loweswater parish!

Mr Wood of Godferhead cared for Crutchy for a year, and then the Skeltons of Foulsyke took him in, and then the Fishers of Cold Keld. But he could not settle down and he moved about the valley from farm to farm, from job to job, eventually returning to Lorton where he worked for a Mr Garnett as 'horseman' because he had a gift with horses. He could be trusted with money, but, as one who knew him said: "to anybody he liked he was as faithful as a spaniel; to anybody he disliked he was as treacherous as a Chinaman and as malicious as an Arab." (The latter two parts of this conglomerate of simile stemmed from difficulties the British were having in Empire-building at the time.)

Crutchy set up as a carter, but his cart was stolen; he married, but his bride left as soon as she discovered that he was not the man of property he said he was, and then he returned to the wild. He lived in haystacks, and used Barty's chair as his principal lair while he conducted a campaign of thieving up and down the valley. He could open any door; he borrowed horses, milked cows, stole hens and eggs, and always got away without the alarm being raised because he was on intimate terms with every farm dog in the district. He eluded trackers by tying a shoe on the end of his crutch – wrong way round, as Barty had done, with one to match on his good foot.

Eventually some stolen property was found in his cave; he was committed for trial by Cockermouth magistrates, sent to prison by the Assize judge, and was heard of no more. In court, his name was given as Will Grave.

The same valley provided a home for 'Hughie' who spent long summer days opening and shutting a gate on Lanthwaite Green for passing motorists, and gratefully accepting the tips they offered for the service. He was one of the pioneers of the gate-opening brigade who appeared on the Lakes scene each spring to make a sort of living opening and shutting gates which had probably been left open all winter. Hughie lived rough in local barns, caused no offence to anybody, always paid his way, and achieved a sort of fame only after his death. At Whitsuntide 1937, at the height of the gate-opening season, Hughie was missing. He was found dead in a barn at Lanthwaite Gate farm. There was no inquest because his death was found to have been from 'natural causes'. On his body were found some documents which answered several questions about him which the dalesfolk, with customary courtesy, had forborne to ask.

First, his occasional affluence was explained by the fact that he was a pensioner of the Canadian Army, having served with them in the Great War. A birth certificate revealed that his surname was McKeown, and that he was born in Whitehaven, although no relatives could be traced. But it was a long, official-looking document, carefully written in immaculate copperplate, which caused clue-questing police to raise their eyebrows. It was headed: "A full account of the great Clare race", and went on to state: "My grandfather was James O'Brian. His mother's name was Gallacher, and my grandfather, born at Killcock, near Dublin, was the son of the King of Ireland in the year 1798, and lost the property."

A few more family details, and the document concluded: "There's a big estate in County Clare, and another near Athlone, and the deeds of the two estates are in my grandfather's name. I am the last descendant of the great Clare race and still carry Royal Descent." Hughie McKeown, sometime of Whitehaven; citizen of Canada; gateman at Lanthwaite Green, and "last descendant of the Kings of Ireland", was buried in a pauper's grave. His gate was never manned again.

The hatchery at Troutdale in operation, from a woodcut in *A Handy Guide to Fish Culture* by J. J. Armistead, 1897

The remains of the fish-rearing tanks of the old Troutdale hatchery

Watendlath, from an engraving by Thomas Allom

Grasmere lake and village. The outline of the rocks on the summit of Helm Crag can be seen faintly on the right. From an engraving by Thomas Allom

"Like a stranded ship . . ." the Bowder Stone stands balanced on its small base. It formerly had a more substantial bed, but 'Squire' Pocklington of Keswick had the surrounding earth removed and turned it into a tourist attraction

2

T' oald fwok were drist in duffel blue,
And t' youngsters in heamm-spun grey,
And nowder were often ower clean or new—
Bit darn't frae day to day.

And o' wad hev brackins or strea in their clogs
Or stickin' ower t' edge o' their shun,
And wad clammer up t' fells, or striddle through bogs:
Od man! but this was laal fun!

And still you believe they war rare oald times,
Far better nor any 'at's new:
So I'll put summat down in canteran rhymes
And than you may judge if it's true.

Their habit o' leevin was poddish at mworn,
And taties and point at neunn:
To let thersels down wi' tea they wad scworn,
So they poddish't at ebnin seunn.

They kilt a fat cow at Martinmas time
And quartert wi' neighbours three;
And except at Kersmas or clippin time,
Fray flesh they wer nar about free

Unless it was bacon, o' reesty and smeuk,
And kizzent and dry't like a sneck,
Till if it fell down outat flags off t' heuk
It wad ring like a pot, or med brek.

In his "Cumberland Farm Life in Old Times", William Dickinson left no doubt that 'poddish' was a staple food. A page from the original manuscript

A tablet to the memory of Canon H. D. Rawnsley and his wife in Crosthwaite church. In addition to proposing a return to the basic diet of long ago, Canon Rawnsley was one of the co-founders of the National Trust

Derwentwater from Castle Head. St Herbert's Island is on the right. From an engraving by Thomas Allom

Ennerdale Water from Smithy Beck

Small as it is, Melbreak nevertheless dominates this view from Loweswater, taken here from Waterend

The Melbreak Foxhounds move off from the Kirkstile Inn. Melbreak is in the background

The Ghyll at Applethwaite: the house, with a few alterations, that Wordsworth built

12

Rent Free, Rate Free and Tax Free

The last chapter dealt with the 'hermits' of the western Lakes, although only St Herbert of Derwentwater could qualify as an undoubted hermit in that he followed the high examples of the founders of the Celtic Christian Church set during the great missionery wanderings which spread the Word through the pagan world of the Roman Empire, and beyond its bounds into the lands of the Pict and Scottish Celts.

Herbert perhaps went a little too far in self-denial in that it is reported that he served penances for himself and for others by standing up to the neck in the icy waters of Derwentwater for hours on end. Apart from this, the tradition says, he did not wash at all, which was not strange in a country where, after the Roman baths had ceased operating, washing 'all over' was not fashionable, or even considered healthy, until quite modern times.

There have been others who could qualify for the description 'hermit' in the terms of less ascetic denizens of the Cumbrian wilds than Herbert of Derwentwater.

Lancelot Pattinson came from the old Pattinson stock of Patterdale and lived a normal life in the parish until his wife died, leaving him with a family to raise. 'Lanty Patty', as he came to be known, moved his family into a cave near Goldrill Bridge which was later named 'Lanty's Castle'. There he brought up his family, and the life must have been healthy enough because he lived to the ripe old age of ninety-five, dying in 1865.

Fred Leake was the last of the Borrowdale 'hermits', living in a rough cave formed under the great jumble of rocks near the road and just outside Big Wood a few hundred yards from where the Watendlath road emerges. He had led a chequered career when he found himself tramping the Lake District and there, captured, he said, "by the incredible beauty of lake and hills", he decided to stop wandering and settle down.

His first cave was in Cat Ghyll and he had been there a year when somebody in authority suggested that as his fire was a risk to Big Wood, he should move. He found his hole in the ground under a great rock below Falcon Crag, enlarged it and made it more or less draught-proof, and set up house with his library, which he kept in biscuit tins. He read Shakespeare, Ruskin, Walt Whitman, Tennyson and Keats, but was "not at all keen" on Wordsworth.

He made many friends, in Keswick as well as among the young people who walked the district in summer and camped near him, and he had a bed under shelter in Keswick when the winter nights became hard to bide.

Not for him a living scraped along on hand-outs or the easy pickings of keeping a gate. He maintained a sort of independence, privacy, freedom, but was outgoing enough to make friends, and when things became tough he consoled himself with Shakespeare's

> Sweet are the uses of adversity . . .
> And in this our life, exempt from public haunt,
> Finds tongues in trees, books in running brooks,
> Stories in stones, and good in everything.

Fred Leake left his Borrowdale cave in the early 1960s. A newspaper story suggesting that he had, in the words of his favourite writer, "shuffled off this mortal coil", drew a sharp retort from somewhere in the Border country – where he had retired from what he called his 'life of vagabondage' – stating in terms of which Mark Twain would have been proud that the report had been greatly exaggerated.

Borrowdale is the heart-land of the Lake Country and it seems to hold a special attraction for people seeking the simple life, a fact which became obvious in the late 1960s when the great cave of Quayfoot quarry developed into a gathering place for youngsters living on the cheap – and Social Security

– in surroundings for which seekers after the peace and quiet of the Lake Country in 'second homes' were paying thousands of pounds for the privilege of enjoying. The Army was called in, not to quell riots, but to dynamite the quarry wall and seal off the cave.

To close off all the available hermits' caves or squatters' roosts in Lakeland would strain the resources of NATO. Millican Dalton had the choice of several, all hidden from the steady stream of foot and car-borne life which flows through Borrowdale. Millican Dalton brings the picture of the Lakeland cave-dweller into flesh-and-blood terms because he is remembered by so many people, and by all of them with affection. He was not a drop-out in the modern sense of the word; he did not cut himself off from the world; he had no grudge against society, no complaints about the Establishment. He simply did not like the idea of living under a roof.

He was born at Nenthead, near Alston, a member of a branch of the Dalton family which sprang from the village communities around Cockermouth, and produced John Dalton, the scientist. The name suggests a connection with the Society of Friends, and Millican was indeed educated at the Friends' School, Wigton. He left that school in 1880, probably for higher education, but 1904 found him working as a clerk in a London office. The life stifled him. He lacked the application, the staying power of the numerous Whittington-esque Cumbrians who went to the Capital and remained to make their fortunes, and so he gave up his job and moved into the Lake Country.

He first came as a guide for the Holiday Fellowship hostel in Borrowdale. Even in that job, spent mainly out of doors, he felt restricted, so, having a small income which he considered sufficient for his needs, he resigned and started camping out. He was one of the originators of lightweight camping, and he designed and made camping equipment to augment his income. He also designed and made rucksacks, and he guided parties of ramblers on the fells and initiated the young and not-so-young into the intricacies of rock climbing.

He was not one of the 'greats' of rock climbing of the Lake District, but he helped Bentley Beetham in his pioneering work on the Borrowdale climbs, finding a kindred spirit in Beetham in sharing a love of life in the great outdoors. His approach to rock climbing was so meticulous, mostly as an example to the young people he was guiding on those so-important first steps in what can be an extremely hazardous pastime, that he "never put a foot wrong". At any rate, as far as can be ascertained, he never had an accident.

An early pupil, Dr Mabel Barker of Caldbeck, was "initiated into the delights of rock climbing" in 1913 by Dalton, who at the time was camping out on a ledge above High Lodore. "He reminded me of pictures of Robinson Crusoe," wrote Miss Barker in her tribute to him in the *Journal* of the Fell and Rock Climbing Club of 1947, the year Millican died at the age of eighty.

He was indeed a spectacular figure. His garb varied a little from time to time, but it was only in slight variations on a theme of Tyrolean hat decorated with a heron's plume, a plaid over a brown tweed jacket, green corduroy shorts and climbing boots. Sometimes he wore stockings, sometimes short socks and encased his legs in puttees.

In 1930 he was established at the foot of Taylor Ghyll Force, living in a little tent and spending much of his time conducting climbing parties on his favourite rocks, the Napes and Kern Knotts on Great Gable. A cold January day in 1941 found Millican Dalton in a cave in House Quarry in Borrowdale, icicles hanging from the roof of the cavern and forming a curtain at the entrance. He had walled in a small section of the huge cave as his personal domain. One corner of this was his sleeping space; his bed was of dried bracken, his plaid was his blanket, and, as a finishing touch and a most unlikely piece of equipment for a cave-dweller, he also had an eiderdown. He was almost apologetic about the eiderdown and admitted to anybody who raised an inquiring eyebrow at the sight of it that it was a "wondrous comfort". In his seventy-fourth year Millican perhaps needed, almost certainly had earned, that little bit of wondrous comfort.

Eiderdown notwithstanding, Millican's accommodation was spartan for a septuagenarian, and he took lightly everything that the unpredictable, even hostile, Cumbrian weather could throw at him and told one caller: "We dress too much. We eat too much. Almost everything we do is too much. Put a man to it, and see what he can put up with." It would seem that, in neglecting to use Millican Dalton and bring his mode of life and asceticism to the notice of a public forced into a life of austerity by the war, the Ministry of Information missed out on a glorious opportunity. His claim that the human frame is capable of withstanding anything the environment holds in store was borne out by the fact that he never had a cold in his life.

For Millican Dalton freedom was everything. "I am as free as the buzzard mewing by day or the owl hooting at night," he said, but he made concessions to control during the 1939-45 war by observing the black-out in his cave. Finding it impossible to make his cave entirely light-proof, he doused his candle at dusk, and during those of the fourteen hours of darkness he was not asleep, lay listening to the sounds of Nature around him: to the barking of the cur dogs at the Borrowdale farms, the sharp yapping of night-courting foxes, the hooting of owls and the whole orchestra of sounds made by falling water.

Living rent-free, with no rates to pay, and no taxes, Millican Dalton was, in his opinion, leading the ideal life. A vegetarian, he found that wartime food shortages did not affect him. He was profound in his belief that man could live by bread alone, with slight adjustments to suit his individual taste. Canon Rawnsley would have loved him, for Millican insisted on wholemeal flour, having a healthy dislike of the over-refined softness of white flour. "The Chinese live on rice," he would say, "so why can't we live on bread?"

To anybody who knew Millican, the question, as he put it, was purely academic because there were few, even among his closest friends, who would argue with him. He was so fixed in his ideas that argument was pointless.

As a guide-line for anybody making his acquaintance,

Millican painted on the wall of his cave the words, "Don't waste words; jump to conclusions", written oblivious to the fact that he had jumped to several conclusions in his lifetime, although it is to his credit that once he had jumped he never budged from the position he had taken.

Most of those who tried Millican's bread agreed that it would be possible to live by that alone. It was of a very special sort. He kept his wholemeal flour in airtight tins. To the flour he added sultanas and currants, a constant supply of which he kept soaking in water in tin containers hanging from the several racks he had constructed for his implements. He added water and made the mixture into a slab of dough about the size of a large grapefruit. He put the dough in a wire cage-like container and hung it over the fire to cook. His fire was the expert outdoor-dweller's fire of biggish logs, nearly smokeless, giving sufficient heat for almost any purpose from a couple of logs generating their fire where they met in a flat bed of white ash.

Everybody who sampled his bread agreed that it tasted good, but "by bread alone" was merely a figure of speech for Millican Dalton. True, wholemeal was the foundation on which he based his diet, but for breakfast he also had porridge, the good old, fast-disappearing oatmeal porridge. But even tough old, back-to-Nature Millican had his reservations about the original porridge. He devised a special way of making it. He put his havermeal first into the frying pan and roasted it before adding water and then bringing it to the boil to thicken to the correct consistency. Then, because he confessed to having "a bit of a sweet tooth", he sweetened it with syrup.[1]

The main meal, dinner in the evening, was again wholemeal bread, freshly made, and potatoes either baked in their jackets or boiled with any other vegetables he could get.

He was not exactly an exponent of 'motion study' methods, but he reckoned that with the methods he used he could, from scratch, cook up to six courses for half-a-dozen people before they started nibbling at the laces of their climbing boots. Simple dishes, he agreed, but he said: "After you have been on the fells all day you can eat anything that is plain and wholesome . . . and a whole lot of it." Nobody who has spent long days in the hills on climbers' 'iron rations' would disagree with that.

His one passion was for coffee, and he considered himself lucky in that he could, for 2*s*. 2*d*. a pound, buy the best coffee he knew, fresh roasted and ground in a Keswick shop. The only way to make coffee, he said, was to use plenty of the raw material and "bring it to the boil three times, but never boil it. Then," he would add, "it's a drink for the connoisseur."

Millican Dalton sitting by his fire, stirring his porridge or baking his bread, or just talking, was a sight to be remembered. His shorts never seem to have been properly finished because they seldom had a hem. He claimed to have beaten Baden Powell by a generation in inventing the shorts as worn by Boy Scouts, but his shorts followed an already well-known pattern, established by the Skiddaw Hermit, even though Millican's were just a little bit shorter.

Some of the aboriginal inhabitants of remoter parts of the world would have found themselves at home with Millican Dalton. He wore boots out of sheer necessity, but took them off, socks as well, at every opportunity, and seldom wore them 'at home'. One of the more startling aspects of Millican at his fireside was his holding his cigarette between the big and first toe of his right foot. Smoking was one of the habits he had got into and could not get out of, and for which he was most apologetic, but his outdoor life must have compensated for his indulgence.

He had a lifelong ambition which was to build a raft and sail it right down from Borrowdale into the Solway Firth, but he never achieved it. He built several rafts to float on Derwentwater, one of them with a small sail, and had to be content with that. On his raft, Millican Dalton presented the picture of the eternal schoolboy enjoying himself.

He lived the life he wanted to live, and he had the means to do just that and no more. A supremely contented man, he was one of a long line of amiable eccentrics to have called the Lake District 'home'.

In his later years, Millican spent his winters, still camping, in Epping Forest, where he had come to 'an arrangement' with the foresters, and he had been missing from the Lakeland scene for some time before he died. He was eighty.

13

Odd Man Out

Keswick, as anybody can see during its now-lengthening season, is not always fortunate in its visitors, but puts on an indulgent face for those who are more 'way out' than average, as long as they do not disturb the peace, and keeps its pursed lips for hikers by posting 'no rucksacks' notices.

Never giving the impression, as most 'tourist' towns do, that it is prepared to sell its soul to the devil of tourism, Keswick has, however, had a longer experience than most places of 'foreign' invasions. In its time it has played host to some turbulent characters. In Tudor times they were the German miners of the 'Mines Royal' and the copper-smelting works at Brigham, who were all but declared undesirable aliens by the locals and had to have an Order In Council from Queen Elizabeth I to protect them from the evil intent of the Keswickians. Then there were the diggers and buyers of illegal 'wadd' who tended to give Keswick a bad official reputation, and the hundreds of Irish labourers who built the railway didn't help much either. More recently there were hundreds of day-trippers from poverty-stricken West Cumberland who came up on Sundays on shilling trips by rail and spent little except a shilling or two in the pubs, which did not make them wildly popular.

However, to its credit, there are very few to whom Keswick has literally 'shown the door'. One of them was the Skiddaw Hermit. Another was Percy Bysshe Shelley. Despite a genius already beginning to glow, a fame starting to show, Shelley seems to have been a less-than-desirable visitor to the town and if he wasn't actually given orders to leave, he interpreted his reception there as being tantamount to orders to quit, and quit he did. He was in fact ordered out of the house he occupied at Chestnut Hill by his landlord – a stout 'statesman' of the name of Gideon Dare – not because he was a drug addict, having become addicted to laudanum with which he dosed himself regularly against the spasmodic pains he said he felt, but because he indulged in pistol practice in the garden, which scared the neighbours, and because he carried out chemical experiments the object of which was to cause explosions which made Mr Dare anxious for the safety of his family and property.

Shelley was born to wealth with £6,000 a year entailed to him, but his father cut him off without even the proverbial shilling for a number of reasons. The first and most important was that Shelley had got himself into trouble at Oxford for writing and publishing a pamphlet entitled 'The Necessity of Atheism'. That, of course, was a swipe at the Establishment of the time which no young, well-connected man was expected to make. The second thing which incurred the displeasure of his father was that at the age of nineteen, against the wishes of his family, he married Harriet Westbrook, daughter of a London coffee-house keeper.

It was a runaway wedding with a difference in that it was the bridegroom and not the bride who was marrying against parental wishes. That the bride's parents approved of the match is shown by the fact that her father allowed them £200 a year, which should have been sufficient to sustain them above the poverty line.[1] With Harriet's sister Eliza in tow they arrived in Keswick in October 1811. Why they chose Keswick is open to question. De Quincey said Shelley was looking for a sequestered place, "which", commented the opium eater, "it was for eight months of the year", and also for a cheap place, which, they were to discover, and De Quincey was later to corroborate, it was not. The truth was probably that at Keswick there was Southey, in whom Shelley expected to find a kindred spirit, and not far away, at Greystoke Castle, was the Duke of Norfolk who was believed to have some influence with Shelley's father.

With only £200 a year at their disposal, their accommodation had to be cheap, but the best they could do was a deal with Gideon Dare, who sounds like the hero of an old-time melodrama and was described by Rawnsley as "as fine a specimen of our Northern yeomen as could be",[2] but was the prototype Lakeland profiteer, and who charged the young runaways two-and-a-half guineas a week for the house at Chestnut Hill, "with linen provided".

Fortunately the couple quickly found friends among the literati who had settled in and around Keswick, but the best friend they made was William Calvert, who owned nearby Windy Brow, and whose brother Raisley, in 1795, had left the £900 to Wordsworth which solved the financial problems of that poet and thereby gave English literature one of its greatest gifts. Without Raisley Calvert's bequest, Wordsworth would probably have entered one of the professions.

In passing one wonders how strong the Calvert influence really was on Wordsworth for, apart from Raisley's bequest in 1795, Wordsworth, anxious and perplexed about his future, went with Dorothy for a short stay with William Calvert in 1794, and at that time probably received at least some good advice from this descendant of the German miners who came to Keswick two-and-a-half centuries earlier.[3]

Wordsworth was not the only poet to get help at Windy Brow. Coleridge went there seeking a home in 1800; in 1803 Southey was a guest, and, about Christmas 1811, Calvert invited Southey from Greta Hall to meet the Shelleys. Shelley had met Calvert at Greystoke Castle when he went there to ask the Duke of Norfolk to intercede on his behalf with his (Shelley's) father because the young poet was running short of money and said he had spent nearly his last guinea on this visit to Greystoke and considered it a poor investment at the time because, as he wrote to a friend, "I have very few hopes of this visit." How right he was! The Duke of Norfolk did intercede with Shelley's father, but without success.

The dividend Shelley drew from his visit to Greystoke was Calvert's friendship. After his visit, Shelley wrote: "We met several people at the Duke's. One in particular struck me. He was an elderly man, who seemed to know all my concerns, and the expression of his face, whenever I held the argument, which I do everywhere,[4] was such as I shall not readily forget. I shall have more to tell of him, for we have met before in these mountains, and his peculiar look struck me and Harriet."

That "peculiar look" must also have struck Wordsworth if, as has been suggested, Calvert was in the poet's mind when he wrote his 'Stanzas in Thomson's "Castle of Indolence" '.

A noticeable man with large grey eyes,
And a pale face that seemed undoubtedly
As if a blooming face it ought to be;
Heavy his low-hung lip did oft appear;
Deprest by weight of musing Phantasy;
Profound his forehead was, though not severe . . .

If the Duke of Norfolk's influence did not succeed with Shelley's father, William Calvert's did with Shelley's landlord because he induced Dare to reduce the rent to a guinea a week. At such a low rent Gideon drew the line at the 'linen included' clause in the agreement he had with Shelley, and so it was arranged that Calvert would lend the young couple some of his own linen.

Chestnut Hill was a single-storey house with a bay window to the room which Shelley used as a study. Its walls were clad with slate and it was adjoined at the end with a cottage which Gideon Dare lived in. The garden was Dare's but he allowed the Shelleys the use of it.

Keswick's reaction to Shelley was normal for a town well acquainted with visitors, but still parochial enough to note such idiosyncrasies as Southey wearing his clogs to church on Sundays and Shelley not going to church at all. "Raything queer in his ways," said the Keswickians of Shelley, as they would of anybody who did not conform to what were regarded as accepted patterns of behaviour, and they were not astonished when word got around that among his strange interests was making explosions and flames in bottles in the garden at Chestnut Hill.

Shelley was working hard and had little time for socializing, or he would have met Southey earlier. On 14 November he was writing; "The scenery here is awfully beautiful . . . but the object most interesting to my feelings is Southey's habitation. He is on a journey. When he returns I will call on him." He must have been very busy indeed or he would have found out that Southey had returned home some time earlier.[5]

On 23 November Shelley was writing to a friend, Miss Hitchener, about a ramble he had taken up Borrowdale, and captured the winter scene with: ". . . these gigantic mountains piled on each other, these waterfalls, these million-shaped clouds tinted by varying colours of innumerable rainbows hanging between yourself and a lake as smooth and dark as a plain of polished jet – oh, these are sights attunable to the contemplation."

That Shelley's heart was not entirely in the Lakes with his young bride is shown in a later sentence of the same letter in which he tells Miss Hitchener: "I have been thinking of you and of human nature. You letter has been the partner of my solitude – or rather I have not been alone, for you have been with me."[6]

Another letter shows that Shelley is now really beginning to enjoy the district. "These mountains are now capped with snow. The lake, as I see it hence, is glassy and calm. Snow vapours, tinted by the loveliest colours of refraction, pass far below the summits of these giant rocks. The scene, even in the winter's sunset, is inexpressively lovely. What will it be in summer?" Shelley was falling under the spell of the Lakes; these were signs that yet another young poet was beginning a love affair with the district, but there were clouds forming on his horizon, no longer rainbow-tinted.

He got his wish and met Southey, and at first found the Laureate "a great man . . . and worthy. In fact, Southey is an advocate of liberty and equality." To Miss Hitchener, Shelley wrote of Southey that he "has all that characterises the poet; great eloquence, though obstinacy of opinion, which arguments are the last things that can shake. He is a man of virtue. He will never belie what he thinks; his professions are in compatability with his practice."

The feeling, apparently, was mutual. "Here", wrote Southey,

> is a young man at Keswick who acts upon me as my own ghost would do. He is just what I was in 1794 . . . Beginning with romances of ghosts and murder, and with poetry at Eton, he passed at Oxford into Metaphysics . . . printed "The Necessity of Atheism"; was expelled in consequence; married a girl of seventeen; and here they are in lodgings living upon £200 a year which her father allows them.
>
> It has surprised him a good deal to meet, for the first time in his life, a man who perfectly understands him . . . I tell him that all the difference between us is that he is nineteen and I am thirty-seven, and I daresay it will not be long before I shall succeed in convincing him that he may be a true philosopher, and do a great deal of good with his £6,000 a year, the thought of which troubles him a good deal more at present than ever the want of sixpence (for I have known such a want) did me.[7]

What happened to change the high opinion young Shelley had quickly formed of Southey? The seeds of the dispute are in Shelley's own assessment of the older man, in "that obstinacy of opinion, which arguments are the last things that can shake . . ."

The young free-thinker, full of the arrogance which he had so widely displayed, simply could not get through the rock-like defences of the conservative Southey, who was probably also at fault in overdoing his indulgence of the youthful impatience of the younger man.

Shelley was also tired. He had worked hard finishing his 'Address to the Irish People' on Catholic emancipation, he was working on his essays, he wrote a number of short poems intended for Irish consumption, and he was also working on a novel. The work took its toll, and to ease the strain and the pain, Shelley took laudanum.

Harriet was involved in an accident on the lake when a boat overturned, and then there was the famous raid on Chestnut Hill on the night of Sunday 19 January 1812. The *Cumberland Pacquet* tells the story:

> Several attempts at robbery have been made within the last fortnight at Keswick and in its neighbourhood, but fortunately without effect. One of the most remarkable was about seven

o'clock on the night of Sunday the 19th inst. at Chesnut Hill, near Keswick, the seat of Gideon Dare esq. A part of the house, it seems, is occupied by Mr Shelley and his family.

Mr Shelley, being alarmed by an unusual noise (but not knowing or suspecting the cause) went to the door; was knocked down by some ruffians and had remained senseless for a time when Mr Dare, hearing the disturbance, rushed out of the house.

The villains, no doubt perceiving that he was armed, fled immediately.

It could not be ascertained how many the gang consisted of, but the attack was of a very formidable nature, and must stimulate the magistrates and inhabitants of the vicinity to make the most speedy exertions and adopt the most effectual measures for the security of the town and neighbourhood.

Whether it was this attack which prompted Shelley to put in some more practice or not is difficult to say. Nor is it certain that the attackers had burglary in mind. This was a time when political passions, particularly on the question of Irish independence and Catholic emancipation, were running high, and when anybody who favoured these issues was unpopular, and particularly so in Cumberland, the western coast of which was in turmoil over these very questions. It could be that the attack was politically motivated; there was no lack of opinion and muscle to plan and carry out such an attack.[8]

Shelley was now openly discontented with his lot at Keswick; disenchanted with Southey when he found out that the man he had idolized both hated the Irish and was against Catholic emancipation. In short, Southey was an "Establishment man".

Besides, Shelley had found a new idol in William Godwin,[9] author of *Political Justice*, and to him Shelley wrote: "Southey, the poet whose principles were pure and elevated once, is now the paid champion of every abuse and absurdity."

The twentieth-century scene of rebellious youth would have suited Shelley down to the ground, but he did not fit into the 1812 Keswick social scene. He ran out of verbal opponents. It might have been different if Coleridge had been around – Coleridge later regretted that he had been absent when this stormy young man arrived: "I might have been of use to him, which Southey could not, for I would have sympathised with his poetics . . . and Shelley would have felt that I understood them."

De Quincey must also have known of Shelley's presence at Keswick, but decided not to put in an appearance and later regretted that he had not shown some attention to a brother Oxonian and a man of letters. "My own library . . . being rich in the wickedest of German speculations would have been more to Shelley's taste than the Spanish library of Southey."

In the meantime Gideon Dare asked Shelley if he would be good enough to find accommodation elsewhere. He was either running out of patience, felt that there was something more sinister than burglary behind the January attack, disliked the idea of a man who fired pistols and made other explosions in the garden . . . or, much more likely, because he saw the Keswick 'season' looming and he with a tenant paying a guinea a week in a two-and-a-half-guinea house.

On Sunday 2 February 1812, Shelley and Harriet, and Eliza Westbrook, left Keswick for Whitehaven to take ship for Ireland. In a letter from "that miserable manufacturing seaport town", which was how he described Whitehaven, written in a "horrible inn" at which he had been staying, Shelley told Miss Hitchener that though they had felt regret at leaving Keswick, "I passed Southey's house without one sting. He is a man who may be amiable in his private character, stained and false as is his public one." He also felt regret at leaving the Calverts, especially Mrs Calvert. And away he sailed from Whitehaven aiming to lead the Irish – or at least point them – towards a new world. He carried with him his hatred of Southey.

Shelley left but a small mark on the many pages given to the literary associations of the Lake Country, and, apart from his dislike of the most illustrious resident of the Lakes at the time, the district left little impression on him – unless it was a memory of that Lakeland cloud scene he described on 23 November 1811, which prompted him to write 'The Cloud'.

> I am the daughter of the earth and water,
>   And the nursling of the sky;
> I pass through the pores of the ocean and shore;

I change, but I cannot die.
For after the rain, when, with never a stain,
The pavilion of Heaven is bare,
And the wind and sunbeams, with their convex gleams,
Build up the blue dome of air,
I silently laugh at my own cenotaph,
And out of the caverns of rain,
Like a child from the womb, like a ghost from the tomb,
I rise and upbuild it again.

He never came back to the Lakes. He died on 8 June 1822, when his boat overturned in a squall in the Gulf of Spezia, Italy.

14

No Ordinary Dog

Not many years ago there was a fox which the Melbreak Foxhounds hunted several times . . . and they never caught it. It was always found at or near the same place, led its pursuers the same merry dance around the same fellsides, forests and fields, and always gave the hounds the slip at the same place.

It might be asked: How did the hunters know it was the same fox every time? But hunters have a way of knowing these things, and the more knowing of the Melbreak supporters just knew that this was the same fox.

The 'cunning' tag attached to the fox is well earned. Foxes have swum rivers to elude their pursuers; they have run railways and roads and even the tops of drystone walls to throw hounds off the scent. A fox has been seen to run round a flock of sheep to gather them into a bunch and then go right through them, exploding the flock to the far corners of the field and put the pursuing pack into a tizzy of uncertainty that required the arrival of the huntsman to sort out.

Eminently adaptable, the foxes today quite often take advantage of the rising tide of traffic in the Lakes to throw hounds off the scent. It sounds inconceivable that a fox should shelter behind traffic, but that, in effect, is what some foxes do. They cross and recross roads, and hounds, being more creatures of habit than their prey, follow the scent blindly and keep their noses down, oblivious of the traffic. The Melbreak Foxhounds lost five hounds in traffic accidents in the 1973-74 season. The traffic did not get a single fox.[1]

In olden days when foxhunting was not organized as it is today, when farmers kept hunting dogs and banded them together for sport when the harvest was in, there was a fox-hunt from Patterdale which belongs to the record books.

Anthony Thompson was tending his sheep when his hound found a fox. The farmer, being busy, let the hound get on with it, and off they went, fox and hound, into the distance. The dog did not return that night, nor was it heard of until the next day, Sunday, when, as the people were coming out of St Patrick's church in Patterdale, the fox, with the dog forty yards behind, ran past. The congregation, parson, men, women and children, joined in the hunt, but half a mile further on the fox, utterly fatigued, gave up and lay down under a gooseberry bush in a garden.[2] The dog came up and lay down beside the fox without even trying to grab him. The fox was killed by a farmer with a pitchfork. The hunt, which must have lasted some 20 hours, was later reported to have been seen over a wide area – at Rydal on the Saturday and at Wythburn and Legburthwaite on the Sunday morning, and one estimate was that the hunt had covered over 200 miles, although, judging from the end of the hunt, it is possible that hunter and hunted had taken some 'time out' from time to time.

Ever after, that particular dog never hunted with the local pack, preferring to take its own road, and usually was in at the death, and often had killed the fox before the other hounds came up.

The craftiest quarry ever hunted in the Lake District was a dog. The Wild Dog of Ennerdale, or, as it is more commonly known, 'The Girt Dog', was no ordinary animal. When caught, it tipped the scale at eight stones. Despite all the arguments which are worked up to justify hunting it – its predilection for such goodies as new-born spring lambs and barnyard fowl, for instance – the fox is held in a sort of regard by the men who hunt it, which is hardly surprising when one has seen hunted foxes up to some of the tricks they use to throw the hounds. The Girt Dog of Ennerdale had no friends; nobody could admit to even a sneaking regard for it. Everybody's hand was against it; every possible hunting method was tried, yet it survived in the fells for four months, killing an estimated 300 sheep and lambs before it finally fell to the gun.[3]

Nobody knew where the dog came from, but he was a huge animal, possibly a cross between a mastiff and a greyhound, and probably an escapee from the chain which had tethered him to a gipsy caravan. He was tawny-coloured, smooth-haired, and had dark streaks in his coat; "tiger fashion", as William Dickinson described it in his *Cumbriana*.

The dog was seen on 10 May 1810 by Mr Mossop of Thornholme. That was probably the time of his arrival in the district because there was no sheep-worrying reported before that date, and plenty afterwards. Mossop told fellow farmers about the huge stray dog he had seen because stray dogs in sheep country were bad news. From the time he was spotted by Mr Mossop until he was shot in September, he was never known to eat anything but mutton, fresh-killed; sometimes, if all the stories about him can be believed, not even waiting for his victim to die before commencing his feast.

Scared away from one sheep he had just brought down, the Girt Dog was found by the shepherd to have torn lumps of living flesh from the poor animal, laying bare the beating heart. On another occasion it ran down a ram and tore flesh from the hindquarters of the animal while it was still able to drag itself forward by its front feet. It not only killed for food; it killed also for pleasure, and could wantonly destroy six or seven sheep in a night. He was seldom seen at his work during the day. Sometimes when he killed at night he would make a lazy, prolonged meal from a single sheep. He was crafty enough not to attack the same flock on two successive nights, often moving two or three miles for his next meal.

With a wild dog at large, local flockmasters were anxious and angry, yet confident that it would soon be caught. It certainly was not the first sheep-worrier they had had in the district. It was the off-season for foxhunting and most of the local foxhounds were at summer quarters, and had put on their summer fat from good living in the farmhouses. It was not unknown for some keen hunter to halloah the hounds together for an impromtu summer hunt, just for the exercise, and so the hounds were called in when there seemed a chance that the Girt Dog would be found. His reaction was to treat the hounds with disdain, for he could have outrun foxhounds in the pink of condition. On one occasion he actually allowed the leading hound to overtake him and then he turned and gave the hound's foreleg such a crushing snap of his powerful jaws that none of the scratch pack would attack him alone.

Flocks were being decimated overnight, and men were out on watch through all the hours of darkness, armed with guns. Hounds patrolled with them in the wild dog's country, but it was generally agreed that no single man or dog could be a match for the Girt Dog and signals were agreed which would concentrate the chase if there was a sighting. The hunter's "View Halloah!" or the firing of a shot was the signal, but the dog seemed to know them as well as the signallers, and was so quickly off the mark and heading for pastures new that sufficient hounds could never be brought forward to engage him with any hope of success.

At one point it was suggested that an attempt should be made to poison the Girt Dog, but that idea died at birth because of the danger to hounds and farm dogs, and because somebody pointed out that the dog had never been known to eat anything but freshly killed meat. Carcases already dead had no attraction for the Girt Dog.

The hunt for the dog disrupted all the operations on the land around Ennerdale. At a time when the men should have been haymaking, clipping sheep or cutting peat, they were out watching for the dog, and their vigil took a toll on family life as wives were disturbed from sleep to provide refreshment for gangs of watchers coming in cold from the fell, and hours of work which should have been filled by the men were done by the women and children. There was no evidence that the Girt Dog was a danger to human life, but the people of Ennerdale were taking no chances, and no child was ever allowed out alone.

The cost in the loss of sheep could be counted, but the loss in work left undone, crops neglected, sleep lost and health impaired could not even be guessed.

In the national newspapers, the story of the wild dog – they called it 'The Worrying Dog of Ennerdale' – ran for weeks, a sensation for the rest of the country, but worrying, in more ways than one, for the people of Ennerdale.

It kept to its Ennerdale territory, which, considering the weight of opposition it was encountering, was strange. If ever it was hunted out of the valley it returned again. It owed its survival to a keen ear, scent and sight. For its laying-up places it chose high ground where it could view a wide stretch of country, and it usually picked terrain where its colour made it indistinguishable from the rocks and yellowing grass around it. Its ultra-keen senses made it impossible for anyone to approach it, for it was quick to sense the approach of the hunter. On the other hand, it was occasionally stumbled upon by accident – the thing seemed to know the difference between a hunter and a casual passer-by – and it never showed any signs of viciousness towards any human who got near it.

One evening the hunters ran him out of the valley and through Loweswater vale where they lost him in the night. Next morning fresh sheep carcases proved that he had quickly returned to his home ground.

On another occasion he was run from the Kinniside fells, by way of Lamplugh and Dean, and, following the example of many a hunted fox, crossed the River Marron several times in the hope of throwing hounds off the scent. He got a good lead on the pack, and was resting up in a wood near Clifton when the hunters and hounds came up and ran him to the Derwent, the hunt being called off after a run of twenty miles. Two days later he was back in Ennerdale; once more the Ennerdale farmers had failed in a bid to present their problem to another district.

The next time he was run, men were posted with guns across the exits from the valley, but he eluded them and killed a sheep.

It was about eleven o'clock one Sunday morning that the men were coming down from the fells after another fruitless night watch when one of them, Willie Lamb, saw the dog, gave the "View Halloah", and soon had the hounds after it.

The hunt passed Ennerdale church when the service was proceeding, but the sound of man and hounds was more attractive than prayer or sermon, and the church quickly emptied, and everybody went after the hunt, the parson included. This run ended at Fitz Mill, Cockermouth, where the dog literally disappeared.

Next morning it was back in Ennerdale where it was spotted by Anthony Atkinson who charged his gun with swan shot and crept slowly up to the dog to make sure of the kill and win the £10 reward which was now being offered to anybody who could rid the valley of its pest. Anthony got a shot in, but the dog got away, not entirely unscathed because some of Anthony's swan shot was found in its hide when it was eventually killed.

The best chance of killing the dog came when he was seen going into a small wood and the hunters were called up to surround it. Men with guns stood ready to shoot, but it was unfortunate for the hunters that it chose to break where Will Rothery was waiting, gun in hand. Will, amazed at the size of the animal, said "Skerse, what a dog!" and stepped aside to allow it to pass, a comfortable pistol shot away. Will was never allowed to forget what he had done.

But the end was near. On 12 September Jonathan Patrickson saw the dog go into a cornfield and said, "Ah'll let tha lig theer a bit me lad." He went quietly away to raise sufficient men to surround the field and when this was done the dog was roused and attempted to break. Only Jonathan Patrickson was near enough to let fly, and his pellets wounded the dog in the hind quarters. This cut the dog's speed, and the hounds which had been brought up were now in full cry and able to keep on terms with him, but always out of range of his powerful jaws. Despite being wounded, the dog gave a tremendous hunt by Kinniside, Eskat, Arlecdon and Asby; by Rowrah and Stockhow Hall down to the River Ehen.

Then a strange thing happened. The wild dog stopped to take a cooling bathe in the river, and the hounds, coming up to the bank stood there, quietly watching him. Then up came John Steel with a loaded gun and the dog made off for Eskatt

Woods. Tired now, he made a few turns to try and throw the hounds, but on one of his turns he came within range and John Steel fired the fatal shot. The carcase of the eight-stone brute was carried back to Ennerdale Bridge, and after most of the people of the district had been to see it, the body was handed over to Hutton's Museum in Keswick where the stuffed skin was exhibited wearing a collar declaring to the world the depredations of the Wild Dog of Ennerdale.

There have been other 'rogue' dogs in the Lakes, but none so damaging or so difficult to catch as Ennerdale's wild dog.

The greatest problem at the present time is that of the 'pet' dog which tries to make sport with sheep, or, much worse, troops of pet dogs on the loose which can do more damage in a few minutes to a flock of sheep than the Girt Dog did in a week.

It never fails to amaze the visitor that hound trails can be run in sheep country: that packs of trail hounds, up to half a hundred in number, can be turned loose to run over eight or nine miles of fell country without their even being tempted to go after any of the many sheep they encounter.

The answer to that is the same as it is to the question why the fell foxhounds never menace the sheep: they are trained not to. The relationship between the Cumbrian sport of hound trailing and farming is so sensitive that the Hound Trailing Association decrees that a hound found sheep-worrying is immediately destroyed, and if a trail hound goes missing after a fell trail, all hound trailing in that area is suspended until the missing hound turns up again.

Not all the animals which return to the wild in the Lakes are dogs. Some time ago there was a goat which roamed the slopes of Yewbarrow in Wasdale, and so ruled the territory which it had appropriated that it stood defiantly in the way of any human intruder to bar his progress, and lowered its head to move into the attack if the intruder failed to get the message.

In case it is thought that all sheep are docile creatures, Herdwick ewes with lambs to guard have been known to send pet dogs cowering behind the skirts of their owners, and, as any shepherd will agree, the best way to cure a dog of the habit of chasing sheep is to tether it to a Herdwick tup which very quickly demonstrates to the dog the error of its ways.

15

The Little Mountain

Melbreak does not qualify for a place in the Top Sixty mountains listed by the Ramblers' Association. Its highest point is a mere 1676 feet above sea level which puts it firmly down among the minnows among Lakeland peaks. Nevertheless it is one of the National Park's most imposing mountains. It impresses because it is one of Lakeland's few free-standing mountains, unattached to any other mountain or range of mountains, which means that it has no loftier sister-peaks for comparison.

The second reason is that despite its size, Melbreak is spectacular, prominent in a most attractice part of the Lakes because it holds the entire southern shore of Crummock Water and dominates that lake as completely as The Screes dominates Wastwater.

Then there is its shape, like a headless sphinx squatting between the Red Pike range and Crummock, with a fine curve of back, and the shoulders a mere eight feet higher than the rump.

It is not particularly favoured by ramblers because there are more glamorous ascents in its neighbourhood, and rock climbers shun it like the plague because, apart from one undistinguished little chimney climb, there is no rock on the entire mountain which is steep enough to present a problem and sound enough to hold a man's weight.

Principal cause for Melbreak's eminence among the Western fells is that it has a pack of foxhounds named after it, an honour shared only by Blencathra, which is only right and proper because both these mountains have names as old as the spoken word, both being formed from the names given them by the earliest inhabitants here.

'Melbreak' is a name which catches the imagination, and on Cumbrian housing estates there are more 'Melbreaks' than 'Dunroamings' or even 'Skiddaws' and 'Scawfells', and when Cockermouth sponsored one of H.M. ships during the 1939-45 war, it was natural that they should choose a Hunt Class destroyer, H.M.S. *Melbreak*.

As will be seen later, the people of the Loweswater valley have been hunters for centuries, hunting with scratch collections of hounds when there was time for sport and relaxation after the harvest. When it was decided to give the pack a firmer footing, and a name, it was natural that the hunters should choose 'Melbreak' because they met at the Kirkstile Inn, and the dominant mountain at that spot is Melbreak, its craggy end seeming almost to have life, towering high one day when the air is crystal clear, lowering and receding a little when a summer haze softens its outlines.

It was natural that the hunters should choose 'Melbreak' for a name because the little mountain is a haunt of foxes, of the lish and lively 'varmints', a bit longer in the leg than the lowland foxes, which can move like the wind on the level and flow up or down a fellside like a windblown leaf.

Foxes choose Melbreak for a 'lie' because they are unlikely to be disturbed there unless the foxhounds are in the district. They can choose between the warm south side of the mountain and the less hospitable north because in neither place are they likely to encounter anything more dangerous to them than Chris Todd's cur dogs going about their business of raking the fellside clear of the Kirkhead flock of sheep. For the same reason Melbreak has long been the resort of the rare birds, great predators like the peregrine falcon and those diligent cleansers of the fellsides, buzzards and ravens.

There were summer days when a dozen buzzards could be seen holding the air above Melbreak, parent birds teaching their young how to use their wings, soaring and circling in the thermals rising from the warm fellside; spring days when the chittering screech of the peregrine was part of the background music to the scene; winter days when an hour could be spent enjoying the antics of courting ravens, which despite their forbidding colour and morbid reputation are amongst the most joyous birds in creation when they find time to play.

The great, blank flank of Melbreak's south dominates the 'hidden' valley of Mosedale, one of several Lakeland valleys so called because there are so many mossy, swampy valleys to earn the name. The very name seemed to have a near-fatal attraction to thirsty local authorities in the immediate post-war years because this Mosedale, as well as the one "back o' Skiddaw" with the Caldew flowing through, was under scrutiny by people visualizing large dams, new lakes and profuse water supplies. At the time the conservationists were not so much angry as amazed that the Loweswater Mosedale should even be considered. There was not quite so much uproar about the Mosedale behind Skiddaw, but fortunately the country ran into one of its recurring financial droughts, and neither valley was dammed, although a 'monitoring' station in the Caldew Mosedale is an ever-present reminder of the threat.

The Crummock side of this saddle-backed mountain runs along the entire south shore of Crummock Water which did succumb to demands for water from Cumberland's west, but has managed to appear unspoiled although the authorities raised the lake level a few feet and dug a new outlet for the River Cocker.

All that remains of feudalism in this area is the name 'Peel', which is a corruption of 'pele', for it was here that the Lindsays, lords of the manor after the Conquest, raised their pele tower. Nothing remains of the little castle, unless the ruins of the old farm incorporate some of its stone. A small rectangular, banked enclosure by the lake shore could have been a fortification of some kind, or a station where the boats from Buttermere could land.

From a distance – from the side of Grasmoor, for instance – the area now called Peel looks like a vast inverted saucer, regular and smooth from the little Crummock beach of pebbles up to the grassy summit where the jewel-like flowers of the heartsease can be found.

Through the ancient, dying oak forest above High Park the footpath emerges on to the fell, with a splendid panorama of Whiteside, Grasmoor and Whiteless Pike spreading out above the rich green of Scale Hill Woods, all reflecting on the face of the clear, cold water.

Along the side of the fell a great dry delta slashes into the scree, an echo, perhaps, of the mighty cloudburst of 9 September 1760 which turned the Liza Beck across the lake into a mighty torrent which spread thousands of tons of rock and stones over the valley down to the Cocker. Some idea of this 'waterspout', as it was called in Hutchinson's *History of Cumberland*, may be gained from inspection of the fellside at the foot of Grasmoor's 'Y' Gully, because the water came down the front of the mountain in such volume and collected at the foot of the gully with such tremendous force that water and stones burst out on to the scree like an explosion and cleared the fellside right down to the virgin rock, baring the great rock steps at the gully foot as if giant excavators had been at work.

And here in the almost equally dramatic moonscape of the dry delta on the side of Melbreak part of the rainstorm fell and lifted a big fan of scree out of the fellside before it ran out of strength and flowed into Crummock.

It is difficult to visualise violence, even of the weather, on Melbreak's side of Crummock.

Higher up on Melbreak's flank is the broken area of red 'pinnacles': red because of an iron content in the rock, 'pinnacles' because of the spiky form of the shivered rock. It is a lonely, haunted place where even the contented 'cronk' of the raven sounds sinister, and the cheerful 'chacking' of the wheatear is seldom heard because that happy little fellside bird likes the sunshine. Here the sun sets early, and from the red pinnacles when the sun has gone, the opposite side of the valley, the sun-soaked, wrinkled face of Grasmoor, and the smiling fields where Rannerdale marches down to the lakeside, are in a different world.

Here among the red pinnacles foxes find refuge when the hounds are after them, and here, in summer, when the hounds are in their holiday homes in the valley farmhouses, the foxes rest and do not expect to be disturbed, which is why this writer has several times come across foxes fast asleep there. The foxes have soon awakened and recovered from surprise, and, generally, retired grudgingly.

Although the Melbreak and the surrounding fells are the haunt of foxes, it is questionable whether the fox is the traditional game of the valley's hunting men. For many years the top-ranking hostelry in the Melbreak Foxhounds' annual itinerary through the western fells, the Kirkstile Inn has an older name, 'The Hare and Hounds', which can be taken as evidence that the hunters of old, described in Houseman's notes to Hutchinson's *History*, were after edible game. Houseman is quoted by Hutchinson as follows:

> Many of the natives are people of property, of course have received a tolerable education, and have been somewhat from home; but I found a number who had been debarred from that enjoyment, and who had seldom travelled beyond their sheep heafs, had seen no people but their neighbours, and no country but their vales and surrounding mountains. Their ideas are simple, and their notions confined to narrow rules of nature; yet honesty, integrity, and heart-felt happiness are no strangers in this sequestered land.
>
> The peasantry have one enjoyment here, which is prohibited to most men of their class. Through the liberality of their lords, a hound is kept in almost every house; two or three qualified inhabitants take licence to kill game and command the pack. As soon as harvest is in, an honest cobbler shifts his garb and becomes huntsman, and every second or third morning collects the dogs, and calls the sportsmen to the field. The cottagers climb the mountainside where they can view the chace, and, without much exertion, enjoy the pleasure of the hunt; after which they retire with chearful minds and invigorated constitutions to their peaceful homes, and do not end the days of sport in revelling and riot, like the sportsmen of the plains. How odious do the game laws appear when held up to this picture of nature!

What a contrast between the lot of the people of Loweswater and their 'liberal' lords, and their neighbours in the Barony of Copeland who, if allowed to keep a dog at all, were ordered by un-liberal lords to lop one foot off the unfortunate animal to prevent it from hunting!

There is not a great deal of difference between the picture Houseman drew of the hunting at Loweswater in the eighteenth century and that of the Melbreak Foxhounds today. Foxes are hunted, and not hare (or deer); huntsman and whip are paid professionals, and in the season the hounds are all kept together at the Hunt kennels, Miller Place.

But in summer the clock is turned back a couple of centuries and the hounds live with farm families to be called in again on Loweswater Show day to start working as a pack. It is one of the annual miracles of Lakeland that fell foxhounds, after spending summer lazily living off the fat of the land and being petted half to death by farm wives and children, can, in a few days, turn back into an efficient hunting pack of hounds.

Another tradition lives on. The Melbreak Hunt's followers still climb the fells to points of vantage from which they can watch the hunting, and some of them, by instinct almost, choose the right place to see more hunting in a day than carborne hunters, who chase up and down the valley roads to the consternation of other traffic, can see in an entire season.

Houseman said that the dalesmen of his time did not end the days of sport in revelling and riot. True, some of them "retire with chearful minds and invigorated constitutions to their peaceful homes", but there are often sounds of revel and riot after end-of-hunt tatie-pot suppers in various pubs in the Melbreak country.

The Melbreak Foxhounds have possibly the longest continuous history of any footpack of fell foxhounds, not always in quest of foxes, but hunting whatever the hounds turned up in the way of game from hares to pine martens, polecats to badgers, foxes to deer.

There is a great deal of criticism of foxhunting today echoing Dr Johnson's immortal castigation in his description of the sport as "the unspeakable chasing the uneatable", but the Lake Country foxhunting carries on without, so far, any protest. The fact that foxes have to be controlled is borne out by the few weeks after the 'official' end of the season when the packs are 'on call' to go after lamb-worriers, which are usually foxes hard pressed at finding food for growing families.

Not only that. Foxes show no signs of decreasing in number despite an annual bag of some 400 foxes a year by the fell packs, along with a considerable toll taken by 'private' hunters entering terriors in fox-holes, and, a few years ago, the depredations of freelance hunters taking scores of fox cubs to be sold as pets.[1]

When John Peel was hunting, that giant among foxhunters did not always kill, or even find. Modern fell footpacks have been known to divide into as many as five different hunts from the same cover at the same time. When John Peel was in his prime, a successful hunt in what is now the Melbreak country was rare enough to warrant a mention in the Cumberland *Pacquet*, and on 12 January 1815 the *Pacquet* reported:

> FOX CHACE. Saturday the 31 ult. the hounds belonging to the gentlemen of Loweswater started, ran and killed two foxes, a male and a female. They also ran a third but were not successful. Their alacrity in these endeavours to extirpate these voracious animals is truly laudable. A subscription to the amount of £8 was raised to defray the expence of an entertainment for the pursuers and for celebrating the exit of Reynard and Reynardine – in many a flowing bowl.

That was a New Year's Eve hunt, but note that the day was Saturday and that hunting on that particular New Year's Day – a Sunday – was unthinkable, as it still is. It was one of many, many "New Eer's Day Hunts at Kurkstee", for that is one of the big days on the Melbreak Foxhounds' calendar when the hunting and the fellowship are good.

A people's hunt, then, is the Melbreak, with ordinary people taking a keen interest in its work, parading proudly their hounds for the 'best-walked' prizes at Loweswater Show before returning them to the kennels for their season's work. A hunt where there is spectator participation; where a follower who knows the rules can "Halloah" the pack to a fox in his view. The fell foxhounds often depend upon such followers for success because the basic idea of the hunt is to kill foxes.

There is a story of a Melbreak follower who went as a guest, on foot of course, to see one of the 'prestige' hunts of the 'Shires' at work. After a check, when the hounds were questing in vain for the scent, he spotted the fox sneaking past him only a few yards away. Helpfully, he halloed the hounds to come, but nothing happened. Later he spoke to his friend at the end of a fruitless day and asked why hounds had not responded to his halloah-ing.

"We do not", said his friend, haughtily, "halloah to hounds here."

"Ye dooan't catch varra many foxes either," said the Cumbrian.

16

The Dream Cottage

One of the first to speak out against despoliation of the Lake District was Wordsworth, which was proper because it was he who drew towards the district the interest which was to swell the volume of visitors and would-be residents to flood proportions in our time and threaten everything which Wordsworth and every other lover of the Lakes held, or holds dear.

Wordsworth has been called two-faced in this matter of conservation because, while he was thundering in protest – in letters to the leading national newspapers – against a proposal to extend Lakeland's thread of the ever-expanding web of railways up to and beyond Windermere, he was also making discreet inquiries as to the wisdom of investing some of his spare cash in railways. It would, however, be stretching the argument too far to call Wordsworth's attitude hypocrisy, otherwise all those members of all the amenities societies might feel honour bound to rid themselves of all their shares in road-building consortia and motor-car manufacturers.

Two-faced or not, Wordsworth could be accused of adopting a dog-in-the-manger attitude where his particular footholds in the Lakes were concerned, and a classic example of this was his exchange with David Lietch of Keswick in 1848, over a plot of land at Applethwaite on the southern flank of Skiddaw.

Wordsworth's early struggles are well documented, if 'struggle' is the correct word for describing a mode of life which the majority of people in his native Cumberland would have considered affluent, and though posterity has sorrowed that a man of such genius should have to endure poverty – even if the poverty was 'genteel' – the pattern of his life was in the mould of that of many other men of genius . . . and there can be little doubt that, as in so many other cases, his best work came when he was, metaphorically speaking, "starving in a garret".

It is perhaps stretching metaphor much too far to equate Dove Cottage with the artist's garret, and indulgence in food prepared by Dorothy and his wife Mary with starvation, but Wordsworth was always convinced that he was born for better things in life than had fallen to his lot at that particular time, and he was fortunate – indeed English literature is fortunate – that there were other people who felt the same about him, and were able to do something about it.

One of these was Sir George Beaumont, whose exertions on the morning of the day of the Waterloo bonfire on Skiddaw had precluded his participating in the evening's celebrations.[1] When Wordsworth's first child, John, was born on 18 June 1803, Sir George, thinking that there might be overcrowding problems at Dove Cottage, presented Wordsworth with a plot of ground at Applethwaite. Beaumont also felt that Wordsworth might welcome a move to Keswick to be near his friends, Southey and Calvert.

A grateful Wordsworth appropriately immortalized Beaumont for his gift with the sonnet 'At Applethwaite':

> Beaumont! it was thy wish that I should rear
> A seemly cottage in this sunny dell,
> On favoured ground, thy gift, where I might dwell
> In neighbourhood with One to me most dear,
> That undivided we from year to year
> Might work in our high Calling – a bright hope
> To which our fancies, mingling, gave free scope
> Till checked by some necessities severe.

That was written in 1804. The 'One to me most dear' was Coleridge; the 'necessities severe' which had checked their 'mingling fancies' being Coleridge's addiction to opium.

Wordsworth might indeed have built his cottage on the land Beaumont had given him had it not been for an early nineteenth-century industrialist Joseph Dover, woollen manufacturer, and his son Joseph, who, to the horror of the lakers, indulged in some industrial development at his Millbeck Mill by erecting buildings of what Southey called "unqualified deformity". Their disgust was at the demolition of some old cottages which had been a part of the usual tourist round of the district.

It is almost certain that Wordsworth's 'Admonition', published in 1807, was aimed at the Millbeck woollen millers, although Wordsworth's note to it says that it was "intended more particularly for the perusal of those who may have happened to be enamoured of some beautiful place of retreat in the Country of the Lake."

> Well may'st thou halt – and gaze with brightening eye!
> The lovely Cottage in the guardian nook
> Hath stirred thee deeply; with its own dear brook,
> Its own small pasture, almost its own sky!
> But covet not the Abode; – forbear to sigh,
> As many do, repining while they look;
> Intruders – who would tear from Nature's book
> This precious leaf, with harsh impiety.

With harsh impiety this precious leaf was torn, and the hamlet of Millbeck was born below Wordsworth's sunny dell, spoiling the view.

In 1848 the woollen industry was in decline, and Dr David Lietch of Keswick came along and gazed "with brightening eye" on this "favoured ground" and thought of building himself a "seemly cottage" there.

David Lietch was born in North Shields, of parents of Scots extraction. Although trained as a doctor, he had journalistic leanings and founded a newspaper *The Tyne Pilot* in North Shields. His idols were Southey and Wordsworth and their influence led him to settle in practice at Keswick whilst still in his thirties. Among his influences on Keswick were the foundation of the famous 'Skiddaw Greys', an elite yeomanry detachment, and the provision of sanitary arrangements for the town vastly superior to those existing on his arrival there.[2]

Poor Lietch! His eye needed some brightening for he was suffering a family bereavement, and, although only forty years old, was considering withdrawal from practice to a life of quiet contemplation of Nature in which he could fulfil his lifelong ambition of becoming a full-time writer. He had plenty of time to look around and, admiring the view from Applethwaite, sought a site for a house there. He found and bought a plot of land in the ghyll above Gale Cottage, about an acre in extent comprising, as Lietch said in a letter to his brother – a solicitor in North Shields, whom David Lietch asked "for a touch of your art in conveying the same" – "two small plots on the skirts of Skiddaw adjudged to two poor men as their share of common right, when the old mountain was enclosed and began to belong, as much as a mountain can, to a man."

An addicted Cumbrian by that time, Lietch considered, however, that his solicitor-brother's 'art' was almost entirely superficial because he had already "after the fashion of these parts" given the 'luck' penny to seal the deal. "Now," he said, "they cannot turn us out of the valley."

Lietch, always receptive of any local lore that came his way, found that the father of one of the old men from whom he had bought the land was one of the first men employed in making the first road "for wheeled vehicles of travel over in this valley, everything previously being conveyed on pack-horses from more civilised lands."

Ardent admirer of Wordsworth that he was, Lietch was probably more delighted than dismayed when he discovered that if and when he built his house on his newly-acquired plot he would be neighbour to the Poet Laureate if that distinguished personage decided to build on the land Beaumont had given him forty-five years earlier.

Lietch could have gone ahead and built his new home; there was nothing to stop him, as there had been nothing to stop Dover building his mill. But the doctor decided that the proper thing to do would be to consult the Poet Laureate in the matter, and the result was an exchange of letters which are interesting.[3]

He told his brother:

> A field and a wooded glen belonging to the poet Wordsworth lie on each side of this little plot of ours, and Wordsworth thirty or

> thirty-five years ago planted a yew, and planned a cottage for himself in this sequestered glen. He will never build one there now, but I have written to ask him if he wishes to do so, for, if so, he will not perhaps like anyone to sit down between his fields, and in that case our cottage vanishes, for the old poet, to whom we all owe so much, must not be displeased.

Wordsworth replied quickly and, assuming that Lietch wished to acquire some of his (Wordsworth's) land, said, "I am sorry that I cannot meet your wishes in respect of parting with any portion of my little property at Applethwaite" which had been endeared to him "by many sacred and personal recollections". He added that he had much regretted the erection of the mill and went on: "Had I known of the intention the fulfilment of which impaired so much of the privacy of the Place, I should have done my utmost . . . to have prevented such an intrusion." Wordsworth told Lietch this had frustrated his original intention of building at Applethwaite, and though at his advanced age he was unlikely to do so that might not be the case with some of his family.

Getting to the nub of the matter, Wordsworth, having failed to prevent the building of the mill, proceeded to frustrate any plans Lietch had by saying that if it was his intention to build on the ground between his two bits of property, he would certainly feel much obliged by his selecting some other spot. Lietch immediately gave in to his idol's wishes. "It is impossible for me to entertain the idea of building a cottage there," he wrote back to the Laureate. He had, he said, bought the land only after being told that Wordsworth had abandoned all intention of building. Not only that, Lietch gave the poet details of the deal in which he had been involved, including the price which had been agreed, and added that he had also had an option on the field above for which the owner would have wanted only a small sum, provided the tenant, an old woman who held it for life, could be persuaded to transfer it.

Lietch no doubt felt honoured at being of some little service to the man he had admired all his life, whom he had never met, or even seen, and felt that some explanation was necessary for what he was sure Wordsworth would have considered an attempted intrusion.

> The reason I so much desired to obtain a resting place, however small and humble, in that dell was that many a time I have carried into it a heart, weary both with bodily pain and the burden of this unintelligible world; and have felt it soothed and relieved by the gentle spirits of this beautiful place; sometimes by the grandeur and beauty of the scene, sometimes by the mingled sounds of the church bells and the running brook which blend there, perhaps more musically than anywhere else in the valley . . .
>
> In fancy I have often seen you in this dell, with those friends who, in early life, often accompanied you there; those great spirits to whom I also owe so much. The idea that among the numbers who have sought this sweet little seclusion for its beauty, there was one who had often sought it in depression, and left it in tranquility, and who loved it the more thoroughly for your sake, will not, I hope, lessen the attachment you have so long and so justly felt for it.

This outpouring did not leave Wordsworth utterly unmoved, and although he delayed his reply for a month, he thanked Lietch, said that he would like to explain in person his reasons for opposing the doctor's plan, and added:

> At present I need only say that my original acquisition of, and subsequent appropriation and long-continued possession of that little property are accompanied with a *sacred* feeling which puts it out of my power to make any change which I can avoid; and I can only say that I exceedingly regret standing in the way of wishes with which I sincerely sympathise.

Wordsworth later took Lietch's advice and acquired the fields, and, his desire no doubt restimulated by Lietch's interest in the place, soon had a cottage built there. Wordsworth never lived in it, but one of his children did. On a brass plate inside was inscribed the sonnet Wordsworth had written for Sir George Beaumont.

Lietch found his new home at Derwent Bank, Portinscale. He never met Wordsworth, but he had a good friend in William Smith,[4] author of *Thorndale* and *Gravehurst*, who came to live near him in 1852, and remained a lifelong friend. Smith married Lucy Cumming, herself a writer, and their friendship meant a great deal to Lietch who obviously had the talent to write, perhaps to make a living out of it, but whose philosophy was probably bound up in those immortal lines of William Smith:

O vex me not with needless cry
Of what the world may think or claim,
Let the sweet life pass sweetly by
The same, the same, and every day the same.

David Ross Lietch died on 16 August 1881, at Silloth where he had gone to try and recuperate from an illness. He was buried in Crosthwaite churchyard, appropriately for anybody who has read such of his work as survives, in 'Poet's Corner', just a couple of yards from Robert Southey.

17

"Es Queer as Dick's Hatband"

Cumberland dialect in its most natural form is a delight. Delivered by one of the world's rarest creatures, a full-blooded Cumbrian untainted by television or radio and unaffected by the accents of off-coming Englishmen, it is like a foreign language except to those born and reared within the sound of it.

Efforts which have been made to preserve the dialect on paper have met with varying degrees of success because it is difficult to produce letter sequences which convey to the reader the broad vowels, the double vowels; sometimes indicate the presence of a word by writing a single consonant of it. The problem is intensified by the contractions, the often misplaced aspirates, the peculiar idiom, strange words, and the strange use of familiar words. In short, the dialect, when attempts have been made to record it faithfully, by such as Alexander Craig Gibson and Thomas Farrall, also *looks* like a foreign language.

And, written or spoken, the true dialect is rapidly becoming 'foreign' even to Cumbrians, because it is disappearing, even in those fastnesses where it held out so long: those mid-western villages of Cumbria which have until recently been leading lives of their own uncontaminated by offcomers. TV, radio, and the rise of a new generation of people, usually educated in the nearest town by people to whom dialect is 'bad' English, have taken their toll of the old speech form.

Natural users of the dialect – and there are a few of them left – are bilingual. They have to be to communicate with the world at large, although the tendency is sometimes to lapse into dialect at awkward moments, as happened recently when a Cumbrian, holidaying of all places in New York, rang for the lift and, when it arrived, bewildered the attendant by asking: "Ista gaan opp er doon?"

All that is best in written dialect has already been printed; the dialect is preserved in an extensive literature in it and about it. People still write in what can be called dialect, but the work of most of them proclaims that the Cumbrian dialect has almost stopped living.

The tendency today is to take a passage of standard English and turn it, almost word for word, into what can pass for 'dialect', but which ignores the fact that dialect, apart from being a speech form which pronounces ordinary words in odd ways – and places particular emphasis on broadening vowels until they are bulbous – has its own words, an idiom entirely its own (including a particularly picturesque simile form), and a grammar which turns the hair of teachers of English prematurely white.

As the simplest of examples, take that most basic of word forms, the verb 'to be': I am, you are, he is, etc. The dialect forms are 'Ah's', 'thoo's', and 'he's' without much emphasis on the aspirate in the third person singular. It is, of course, possible to hear a dialect speaker say "Ah'm gaan", for "I am going", which would be grammatically correct English translated into dialect, but much the commoner form, "Ah's gaan", translates into "I is going", which is not what the average English teacher wishes to hear, any more than "Thoo's gaan", which translates into "You is going" and would be placed in the cotton plantations of America's deep south rather than in a mining village in West Cumberland.

But the dialect form of that very simple verb is not so very wrong if we relate it to the German form of the same verb. The German second-person singular 'polite' form is "Sie sind" which translates easily into "you are"; the 'familiar' form, "du bist", translates equally easily into the Cumbrian "thoo's".

The dialect greeting "Hoo ista?" ("How are you?") is answered by "Ah's gaily weel" ("I am very well"), or "Ah's nobbut a bad fettle" ("I am not so well"), which is the simplest of simple exchanges between Cumbrians, but which would have the unaccustomed off-comer bewildered.

"Ah'll off an' lait me gripe" says the true Cumbrian, indicating that he is going to get his garden fork, and if at Loweswater show or Grasmere Sports he is introduced to somebody who bears the same surname (and some surnames have spread themselves all over Cumbria), he'll ask, "Ista owt a-keen?" which is the Cumbrian way of asking whether there is any family relationship between them.

The old dialects of Cumbria related to districts, so that a Wigton person could identify a Carlisle person by the way he or she talked, and it was the same between coastal towns, inland villages and the hamlets of the dales. It is still possible to identify a Carlisle Cumbrian from the pronunciation of the city's name, which usually comes out as something like 'Ceyleyle', and whereas the native Cumbrians of other districts use the truly English orthodox 'like', the Carliol will say 'leyke', which makes it obvious to anybody who has read his dialect work that Robert Anderson, "the Cumberland Bard", was a Carlisle man.

The west Cumbrian dialects were polluted by the infusion of other dialects when West Cumberland's industrial revolution led to the importation of labour from Ireland, Scotland, Northumbria, Lancashire and even Cornwall which produced hard-rock miners for the hematite ore mines. Workington had an entire community of Dronfielders imported from the Derbyshire town with Cammell's steelworks, and a Welsh colony with the Barepot tinplate works.

All these invasions made their contribution to local speech forms, today described as 'dialect', although Whitehaven's 'marras' and the shout of 'howay' belong more to Northumberland than to Cumberland.

The spoken dialects of the west coast and the inland mining villages are harsh and designed for argument; in the dales of the Lake Country the dialect is softer, easier on the ear, a language designed for the telling of tales.

The trouble today is that few people take the dialect

seriously. Those to whom it is the natural way of speech do not see anything funny in it, although they are usually quick to detect an interest and can keep going for hours and turn trivial incidents into sagas.

Dialect today suffers a hangover from a long line of writers who put it down on paper, in prose and in verse, and found a rich vein of broad, often simple humour which diverted those who read or heard it. It still does and there are many entertainers of Women's Institutes who have learned 'Betty Wilson's Cummerlan' Teals' off by heart.

Many who have lived with the dialect all their lives cannot see it as the language of romance, and believe that it is not possible to express affection or undying love in it. Maybe so, because the Cumbrian is, as a rule, undemonstrative; but John Richardson, of St John's in the Vale,[1] told a love story in 'It's nobbut me', and Josiah Relph, of Sebergham, the 'father' of Cumbrian dialect poetry, showed the way to romance with 'Bonny Smurkin' Sally', and lightsome, homely humour in 'Ae day as cupid'.

> Ae time as Cupid sweet-tooth'd fairy
> A hive, owre ventersome, wad herry;
> A bee was nettled at the wrang,
> And gave his hand a despart stang;
> It stoundit sair, and sair it swell'd,
> He puff'd and stamped and flang and yell'd;
> Then 'way full drive to mammy scowr't,
> And held her't up to blow't and cur't,
> Wondrin' sae feckless-like a varment
> Could have sae fearfu' mickle harm in't.
>
> She smurk'd – and pra' tha' says his mudder,
> Is not lile Cupid sec anudder?
> Just sec anudder varment's he;
> A feckless-like – but fearfu' bee.

However, the greatest weight of dialect writing, and especially of poetry, has gone into the epics about communal celebration such as John Stagg's 'Bridewain' which set the fashion, and 'Rosley Fair' which is a document of the manner of bygone Cumbria; Mark Lonsdale's 'The Upshot', Robert Anderson's 'Worton Wedding' and 'Bleckwell Murry Neet', and other racy pieces about countrymen (and women) letting their hair down.

It was, perhaps, right and proper that early writers of dialect should choose such activities for their subjects as more suitable to what Craig Gibson called "the harshness of cadence" of the dialect,[2] but some of the earlier writers, albeit in diluted dialect, did manage to sing convincingly of love and tenderness.

Susannah Blamire wrote 'What ails this heart o' mine?' in what can be called 'watered-down' dialect, which probably accounts for it becoming a popular song of its time:

What ails this heart o' mine?
What ails this watery ee?
What gars me a turn cauld as death
When I take leave o' thee?
When thou art far awa'
Thou'lt dearer grow to me,
But change o' place and change o' folk
May gar thy fancy jee.

When I gae oot at e'en,
Or walk at morning air,
Ilk rustling bush will seem to say
I us'd to meet thee there;
Then I'll sit down and cry,
And live aneath the tree,
And when a leaf fa's i' my lap
I'll ca't a word frae thee.

As dialect, this poem, in the Cumbrian idiom, is "nowder nowt nor summat", but it is easy to recognize the real Carlisle district dialect in her 'We've hed sec a durdem', the first verse of which goes:

We've hed sec a durdem at Gobbleston parish,
For twenty lang years there's nit been sec a fair;
We'd slack reape, and tight reape, and dogs that were dancin',
Wi' leytle roun' hats on to gar the fwok stare;
A leytle black messet danced sae like auld Jenny,
I thought it wad niver rin out o' my head;
It was last thing at neet, and the first i' the mwornin',
I roared like a feul as I laid i' my bed.

Of modern dialect writers there has been none to equal the

late William Sanderson, of Aspatria, and later of Keswick, in either poetry or prose, but he was a dialect purist and to anybody but a Cumbrian with a good eye and ear for, and memory of, the dialect, his work is almost unintelligible. Take his description of 'T' Rheumatic':

> Help't bih a strang esh kebby-stick
> (Pass't on teh son frae fadder).
> He hokker't doon teh t' lonnin'-en',
> A fave'rit gedderen-spot fer t' men
> Teh sit an' smeuk an' bladder.

Delightful (to the enthusiast) as the dialect poetry is, prose gives fuller reign to the creative writer, and it was Alexander Craig Gibson who opened the door to a whole new area of Cumbrian literature when in his *Folk Speech of Cumberland and some Districts Adjacent* he laid down guidelines for dialect spelling which are followed to this day. Gibson's name as a dialect writer was made by his 'Joe and the Geologist', which Sidney Gilpin described as "by far the cleverest prose composition we have in the dialect", a compliment which was amply repaid when Gibson allowed Gilpin first publication rights on 'Lal Dinah Grayson', which is one of the best songs in the dialect.

Because it was a milestone in dialect writing, 'Joe and the Geologist' is worth re-telling:

> Ya het foorneun, when we were oa' gaily thrang at heam, an oald gentleman mak of a fellow com' in tul ooar foald an' said, whyte nateral, 'at he wantit somebody to ga wid him on't fells.
>
> We oa' stopt an' teuk a gud leuk at him afoor anybody spak; at last fadder said, middlin' sharp-like – (he oalas speaks that way when we're owte sa thrang, does fadder) – 'We've summat else to deu here nor ga rakin' ower t' fells iv a fine day like this, wid neabody kens whoa.'
>
> T' gentleman was a queerish like oald chap wid a sharp leuk oot, grey hair and a smo' feace – drist i' black, wid a white neckcloth like a parson, an' a pair o' specks on t'top of a gay lang nwose at wasn't set varra fair atween t' e'en on him, sooa 'at when he leukt ebben at yan through his specks he rayder turn't his feace to t'ya side.
>
> He leuk't that way at fadder, gev a lal chearful bit of a laugh an' said, iv his own mak' o' toke, 'at he didn't want to hinder wark, but he was give anybody 'at ken't fells weel a matter o' five

shillin' to ga wid him, an' carry two lal bags.

'Howay wid tha, Joe,' sez fadder to me, 'it's a croon mair nor ivver thou was wurth at heam.'

I mead nea words aboot it, but gat me-sel a gud lump of a stick, an' away we set, t' oald lang-nwost man an' me, ebben up t' deal.

As we war climmin' t' fell breist, he geh me two empty bags to carry, mead o' ledder. Thinks I to mesel, 'I's gan to eddle me five shillin' middlin' cannily.' I nivver thowte he wad finnd owt on t' fells to full his lal bags wid, but I was mistean!

He turned oot to be a far lisher oald chap nor a body wad ha' thowte, to leuk at his gray hair and his white hankcher an' his specks. He went lowpin' owre wet spots and gurt steans, an' scrafflin' across crags an' screes, tul yan wad ha' sworn he was summat akin tul a Herdwick tup.

Efter a while he begon leukin' hard at oa' t' steans an' craggs we com' at, an' than he teuk till breackan lumps off them wid a queer lal hammer he hed wid him, an' stuffin' t' bits intil t' bags 'at he geh me to carry. He fairly capp't me noo. I dudn't ken what to mek o' sec a customer as this.

At last I cudn't help axin' him what mead him cum sea far up on t' fell to lait bits o' steans when he may'd finnd sea many doon i' t' deals?

He laughed a gay bit, an' than went on knappin' away wid his lal hammer, an' said he was a jolly jist.

Thinks I to mesell, thou's a jolly jackass, but it maks nea matter to me if thou nobbut pays me t' five shillin' thoo promised ma.

Varra weel, he keep't on at this feckless wark tul gaily leat on i' t' efter-neun, an' be that time o' day he'd pang'd beath o' t' ledder pwoakes as full as they wad hod wid bits o stean.

I've nit sea often hed a harder darrack efter t' sheep, owther at clippin' time or soavin' time, as I hed followin' that oal grey heidit chap an' carryin' his ledder bags.

But hooivver, we gat back tul oor hoose afoor neet. Mudder gev t' oald jolly gist, as he co't hissel', some breid an' milk, an' efter he'd tean that an' toak't a lal bit wid fadder aboot sheep farming an' sec like, he pait ma me five shillin's like a man, an' then tell't ma he wad gi' ma udder five shillin' if I wad bring his pwoakes full o' steans doon to Skeal Hill be nine o'clock i' t' mwornin'.

He set off to woak to Skeal Hill just as it was growin' dark; an' neist mwornin', as seun as I'd gitten me poddish, I teuk t' seam rwoad wid his ledder bags ower me shoolder, thinkin' tul me-sel' 'at yan may'd make a lal fortune oot o' thur jolly jists if a lock mair on them wad no' but come oor way.

It was anudder het mwornin', an' I hedn't woak't far till I

begon to think that I was as gurt a feul as t' oald jolly jist to carry brocken steans o' t' way to Skeel Hill, when I may'd finnd plenty iv any rwoad side, clwose to t' spot I was tackin' them tul. Sooa I shack't them oot o' t' pwokes, an' then stept on a gay bit leeter widout them.

When I com bar to Skeal Hill, I fund old Aberran Atchisson sittin' on a steul breckan steans to men' rwoads wid, an' I as't him if I med full my ledder pwoakes frae his heap.

Aberran wasn't varra kaim't an' tell't ma to tak them 'at wasn't brocken if I wantit steans, sooa I tell't him hoo it was an oa' aboot it.

T' oald maizlin was like to toytle off his steul wid laughin', an' said me mudder sud tak gud care on ma, for I was ower sharp a chap to leeve varra lang i' this warld; but I'd better full my pwoakes as I liked, an' mak on wid them.

T' jolly jist hed just gitten his breakfast when I gat to Skeal Hill, an' they teuk me intil t' parlour tul him. He gurned oa't feace ower when I went in wid his bags, an' tell't me to set them doon in a neuk, an' than ax't ma if I wad hev some breakfast.

I said I'd gitten me poddish, but I dudn't mind; sooa he tell't them to bring in some mair coffee, an' eggs an' ham, an' twoasted breid an' stuff, an' I gat sec a breakfast as I nivver seed i' my time, while t' oald gentleman was gittin' his-sel' ruddy to gang off in a carriage 'at was waiting at t' dooar for him.

When he com doon stairs he geh me t'udder five shillin' an' pait for my breakfast an' what he'd gitten his-sel. Than he tell't me to put t' ledder bags wid t' steans in them on beside t' driver's feet, an' in he gat, an' laugh't an' noddit, an' away he went.

I nivver owder seed nor heer'd mair of t' oald jolly jist, but I've offen thowte there mun be parlish few steans i' his country, when he was sooa pleas't at gittin' two lal ledder bags full for ten shillin', an' sec a breakfast as that an'.

It wad ve a faymish job if fadder could sell o' t' steans iv oor fell at five shilling a pwokeful – wadn't it?[3]

'Joe and the Geologist' became very popular, and in the ways of the time, Gibson soon had copiers, and an anonymous writer in the *Whitehaven Herald* wrote a supplement to the story. This, afterwards published as a pamphlet, represented Joe as a knave, so Gibson went into print again with his own sequel, written to dispel any illusion which the original story might have put afoot that the Cumbrian was a rogue. The plot of the sequel was as simple as that of the original. Joe's 'fadder' had heard that the 'jolly jist' had turned up at Scale

Hill again, and since old Aberran Atchisson had another good heap of stones ready broken beside Kirkgate, he thought he might do some more business with him. So, innocently – or as bold as brass, whichever way you look at it – Joe returned to Scale Hill, and, to cut a long story short, eventually returned the rock samples to the 'jolly jist' (because he remembered where he'd tipped them out) and got another five shillings for being honest about it!

There is an intimacy about dialect writing that is rather touching. Post-Gibson writers about dialect have gone to some trouble to examine the character of Joe, of 'Joe and the Geologist', as if he was a real person (one of the Denwoods dismissed him as a 'hofe-thick'), and the same sort of post-mortem has been held on another of Gibson's anti-heroes, Bobby of 'Bobby Banks's Bodderment', which ended with that fictional character slightly stained as well.

Whatever form it takes, poetry or prose, comic or serious, there can be no denying that, except in the remoter dales where it still hangs on by a thread, Cumbrian dialect, as Craig Gibson said, is hard and coarse.

18

Central Buttress

Rock climbing has gone through several phases since the British first introduced the pastime to a society hungry for exciting things to do. After the first discovery that there was a thrill to be got out of risking one's neck climbing difficult and more difficult routes to the tops of crags for no reason which was apparent to the casual observer, the climbers started to introduce variations on the theme of upward, difficult progression.

First there was the widening of the scope of the pastime: the finding of new routes, new crags and new mountains, the last-named quest culminating in the farthest-flung corners of the earth.

Then there was the development of equipment from the first primitive boots, nails and alpenstocks; and dress from the casual Norfolk-jacket-type gear to the purely functional and nigh indestructible garb which was to become the climbers' uniform.

And along the line, in every phase, there were, watching from the sidelines, the dedicated climbing traditionalists tut-tutting at every innovation, every departure from what they thought was acceptable procedure.

And throughout the history of the sport its devotees were considered by more sedate contemporaries to be rather more than slightly mad. It was almost, at times, as though the climber was indulging in illicit thrills because he tended to be rather secretive; he seldom advertised the fact that he was a rock climber; he would go to the spot selected as the start point of a climbing expedition in conservative dress, and only emerge complete with nailed boots and climbing rope on to the fellside.

It was an extremely sensitive area of sport in those early 1930s, when the writer first became involved, because the biggest headlines of half a decade had heralded the fact that King Albert of the Belgians had got himself killed whilst rock climbing, and that sort of thing preyed on the public mind. Rock climbing did not countenance show-offs – and that term included everything from the fellow who wore nailed boots and slung rope in Keswick's Main Street declaring to the world that he was a climber, to the out-and-out publicity seeker, of whom there were a few about.

Rock climbing was a sort of closed shop, and, because of its mostly unwritten rules, the Fell and Rock Climbing Club was one of the more exclusive organizations. For the tyro, membership of the 'Fell and Rock' was somewhere over the most distant of horizons; one assumed that it would be much easier getting into Heaven.[1]

H.M. Bateman never did, but he should have drawn one of his famous cartoons entitled 'The Man who used a Piton'. Only that famous cartoonist could portray the looks of absolute horror which would have appeared on the faces of listeners to his confession in the Wastwater Hotel, for although guests at that famous hostelry could indulge in such pranks as the 'Billiards Table Traverse', none would have ever fallen so low as to use an 'artificial aid' to climbing.

On Boxing Day 1892, J.N. Collie, stymied at the exit from the big cave when endeavouring a first ascent of Scafell's famous Moss Ghyll, chipped a foothold in the rock with an ice axe, a definite breach of the unwritten law, and the mind boggles at what the consequences would have been in the corridors of power of the 'Fell and Rock' if he had not, with this aberration, presented the sport with one of the finest gully climbs in England.

It was the first recorded use of an artificial aid in rock climbing. Climbers were expected to get up without such aids, by using the powers God had given them, of muscle and of balance, and this writer's introduction to rock climbing came at a time when the 'purists' sneered a bit even at climbers who wore 'rubbers' – gymn shoes, or 'plimsolls' – to climb the more delicate rock problems, the term 'rock gymnasts' being bandied about by the older hands at the game.

Seismic instruments probably went haywire recording earth movements caused by rock climbing pioneers turning in their graves when post-war generations of climbers introduced the regular use of the piton, even if that devilish instrument did open an entirely new field to the climbing fraternity. Old-timers who looked with suspicion at the safety-promoting carabiner would be paralysed with horror at the thought of a veritable armoury of ironmongery now in regular use by rock climbers. They would avert their eyes from sights to be seen in the streets of Keswick and on tracks leading to rock-climbing localities of young men wrapped in coils of rope – rope! we called that stuff 'line' – and decorated like Christmas trees in chains of carabiners, bunches of pitons, bundles of wire ladders, loops, stirrups and hammers. It is traumatic even for such an undedicated climber as this writer to see such things, remembering, as he does, that the sport was – when he took his first uncertain steps up Grasmoor Gully – still in a state of shock from Collie cutting that step forty years earlier.

Nowadays the 'Fell and Rock' actually publishes guides which not only recommend the use of pitons on certain climbs, but actually mentions places where pitons are fixed, apparently for ever! Shades of Owen Glynne Jones and H.M. Kelly![2]

The nearest this writer ever came to using artificial aids was a surreptitious haul on the rope when the hand- and foot-holds were too small – and when nobody was looking – and indulging in a few moments of relaxation in the slings at the chockstone of the Flake Crack on Central Buttress, Scafell.[3]

It says something for the dedication of the 'purist' rock climber of those good old days that our leader, sometimes reluctantly, had to issue such advice as "Feel a bit up there on the left; there are some roughnesses on the rock which will help." When it is made clear that that was to a climber 'backing up' in the chimney of Deirbield Crack in Easdale, whose opposing smooth sides narrow towards the top, it will be realized that the leader wasn't helping much. It is not to be wondered, in that sort of atmosphere, that this writer (who had gratefully opted out of that particular climb and was dashing round taking photographs with a quarter-plate reflex camera just a little smaller than the life-support systems carried by men on lunar landings) was rather reluctant to offer advice on the final pitch. The leader was struggling, which was a strange experience for him. He was near the top and couldn't find a last hand-hold. This writer was viewing operations from above and could see a hand-hold about the size of a jug handle, and it took a great deal of self-examination on my part – and the realization that the leader was on the point of falling off through sheer exhaustion and exasperation – before I asked, rather timidly, if it would be against the rules to tell him that there was a great big hand-hold just a few inches north of his forehead. I gathered afterwards that that information would have been much more welcome if it had been given earlier.

It was an extraordinarily conservative education in rock climbing that beginners undertook in those days. One didn't feel 'dashing' about it; one wasn't expected to boast about it; and, although a journalist all my life, I was reluctant to write about it, and especially about rock and fell 'incidents' which the national Press tended to blow up into disaster proportions. Ropes were kept hidden in rucksacks until we were actually on the fell, and we would have as soon gone to a dance in our nailed climbing boots as walked the streets of Keswick in them.

We were sometimes caught unawares, as on that memorable day when leaving civilization behind at Burnthwaite and venturing into the untamed wild of Sty Head, we, in boots, and encumbered with ropes and rucksacks, encountered a pair of elderly ladies who lifted their hands in horror and exclaimed: "Oh! Going roping! How exciting, but how dangerous!" I can't remember whether it made our day or spoiled it.

My unfortunately short career in rock climbing had its

highlights, but descended occasionally into the bathetic as when a clumsy fall on Kern Knotts Crack ended, miraculously with me on my feet in the Sentry Box, in a round of unstinted applause from a watching crowd of hikers which was rather surprising because we always felt that passing hikers only paused to watch in the hope that one of us would fall and break a limb.[4]

The highlight of highlights was a fortnight spent camping on Wasdale Head Hall ground during which we skimmed the cream off what was then considered to be the definitive list of Scafell and Great Gable rock climbs. Shining like the brightest of bright stars in the modest galaxy of my rock-climbing achievements was the day we climbed Central Buttress. Central Buttress, or 'C.B.' to anybody who can claim close acquaintance with it, is – and I quote the guide of the F.R.C.C. (1974 edition) – "probably the most famous climb in Lakeland". It consists of 475 feet of rock climbing of extreme severity, and – again quoting the F.R.C.C. guide – the first ascent in 1914 was "probably the biggest single breakthrough in standard in the history of Lakeland climbing". For us it was the ultimate in climbing: the final goal, having achieved all those other dreams – milestones, call them what you will – like Pillar Rock summit, Napes Needle, Kern Knotts Crack, Walker's Gully.

We had been blessed with the better sort of Wasdale Head weather (there are only two sorts: good and bad), and though spurred on by the leader of the party who had by now, being far more dedicated to the sport than anybody else I was ever likely to know, scaled just about everything in most of the Fell and Rock guides, we had a tendency towards idleness in the sun rather than tigrishness on the rocks.

It was definitely a Napes or Kern Knotts day, those sun-soaked crags being most attractive on the better days of summer. We went up Eagle's Nest, and were making a leisurely way down by way of Eagles Nest Chimney when who should we meet but Mabel Barker – Doctor M.M. Barker, of Friar Row, Caldbeck, a true 'personality' of the fells, who was climbing the Chimney in company with a young Swiss girl, who was being initiated into the delights of rock climbing just as Mabel herself had been introduced to the sport twenty-three years earlier by Millican Dalton.

A stranger to the sport might think it unlikely that people could actually 'meet' on rock climbs, and even less likely that in such conditions long and pleasant conversations should develop. But, rock climbing being (then) a chummy sport, that is what happened that fine, sunny day in 1934.

Seemingly idle chatter led to the revelation that the following day would be Mabel's fiftieth birthday and that, as the first woman to climb C.B., she would also like to climb it on her fiftieth birthday. Mabel droppped hints to this effect like blows from a sledgehammer, but, being a most obliging lad, our leader volunteered to lead Mabel and the rest of us up C.B. the next day.

Mabel was camping at Seathwaite; Alan Horn of Edinburgh, who was also in our party, was camping with his mother at Wasdale Head. My camping companions were Jack Carswell and Austin Barton. Jack and I had shared that first youthful essay up Grasmoor Gully, and he had, at a remarkably early age, attained considerable stature as a rock climber, a stature which was to increase as the years flowed by. Austin was a skilful climber but more dedicated, perhaps, to his other hobby, photography, mainly of Lakeland's birds of prey.

We decided to meet at Sty Head Summit. Time, we also agreed, was of the essence, and so, with fervent promises that we would be on time, we parted. It must be some sort of a record that we all turned up on time, and, following the Corridor route, headed for Scafell Crag.

Although there were six of us in the party – Miss Barker had brought the Swiss girl, Hedi, with her – it was early decided that no more than five should climb C.B., and, with five on the rope, we knew we would have to allow plenty of time.

That notwithstanding, we wasted time on an outcrop of rock on Round How, discovering new, unconquered routes which never made it into the F.R.C.C. guide-books for the simple reason that they were almost horizontal. It was that sort of a glorious, sunny, lazy day.

At the foot of C.B. there was no dispute when Hedi was left off the climbing party, and disappeared over the Pike, yodelling.

There was no dispute about leadership either: Jack, because he'd climbed it before. To overcome C.B.'s greatest problem, the Flake Crack, it was necessary that the second should also be a good climber, so Alan Horn was elected – naturally, because he had won an undying fame by climbing the Innominate Crack on Kern Knotts in nailed boots![5] In the middle came Mabel Barker, and I was fourth on the rope. In the unenviable position of last man, came Austin.

We started climbing, and quite early decided – those of us who hadn't climbed C.B. before – that it was everything it had been made out to be.

After two pitches we arrived at The Oval, named not for its shape but after the Cricket ground of that name, because that's how big it looks as soon as you have left it.

We followed the 'book' – the F.R.C.C. guides, and anything else that issued from that august body and which was available to the general public (of which we were members) were treated as Holy Writ. Alan led to the first chockstone at the foot of the Great Flake, and tied on. Jack followed and led through up the almost invisible 'holds' of the Flake Crack (I believe that it is treated as a lay-back today) to the large chockstone. Here he tied on and arranged a 'cradle' of rope slings in which he sat while Alan climbed up to and over him to the top of the Flake.

Soon we were all seated on the Great Flake, an enormous flake of rock, weathered so thin at its top that there is a hole in it. Not the most comfortable seat, but we endured it for a long time for the sheer novelty of it: five of us sitting there carrying out tests to see if it was true that you could spit from the top of the Flake to the scree below. It was true.

We were, of course, wasting time, and in that time changes were taking place in the weather. While we watched, the sky reddened in the west in one of those livid Turneresque sunsets, and, unseen, a cloud crept up Eskdale. We became suddenly aware that a great thick mist, tinted pink by the setting sun, was pouring over Mickledore, and, borne only by its weight – for it was a windless evening – was beginning to roll down and fill Hollow Stones. The mist began to rise, and soon we were engulfed in it. Darkness fell with tropical suddenness, and, although we had made rapid progress, we were left with a few pitches to climb in the dark. It was not easy, least of all for Jack, but he got us up safely, and showed us the way down Broad Stand where our food reserve was stored: one small piece of cake among the five of us.

Hollow Stones in daylight is interesting and quite spectacular. In darkness it is a labyrinth, and we bumped into the bigger stones and fell over the smaller ones. We were ill equipped for such a situation: not an electric torch amongst us, and only half a box of matches. We used up the matches getting clear of the hazards of Hollow Stones, and were making quite good time down the fellside in inky blackness when Alan urgently called a halt.

In a matter-of-fact voice, he said, "If we are on Brown Tongue, where we ought to be, we should be able to hear a beck on our left, shouldn't we?"

We agreed, and then we listened very intently, only to discover that a beck could be heard on our right, but that to our left there was nothing but dead silence.

It became imperative that we should find the beck on our right, and cross it, and it was agreed that caution was necessary because we didn't know what lay between us and the beck.

We found the beck and fell into it, and drank of it gratefully. We plodded on and found the Brown Tongue footpath, well worn and therefore easily recognized in the dark.

We toiled on through velvet-black darkness, saw some lights which turned out to be glow-worms in a mossy bank, and breathed sighs of relief when Wasdale Head's few lights hove into view. Home, we thought; not dry because we were soaked by falling into the beck and by the precipitation from the thick mist, but home nevertheless.

One of the lights was bobbing along the road from Wasdale Head in the direction of Wasdale Head Hall.

"That", said Alan, "is mother, going to your camp, looking for me."

He shouted "Mo-ther", but there was no response. Then all five of us in unison called "Mo-ther" which raised a faint echo from Yewbarrow. The bobbing light stopped and shone towards us; and then it began to retrace a course back to Wasdale Head. We plodded wearily down.

There are several stiles to negotiate from that point, and this was not made any easier by Alan's mother, trying to be helpful, turning the car and shining its powerful headlights up the fell and right into our eyes.

Realizing that over at Seathwaite they might be worrying about her, Mabel declared her intention of setting off alone over the Sty, an intention which was frustrated by Alan offering to take her round – via Gosforth, Egremont, Cockermouth and Keswick – by car.

It is a sobering thought that, although we had done everything 'by the book', we had not only wasted time, but had not initially allowed sufficient time for such a climb. In retrospect, we can smile at this adventure; take a leap in time to the present day, and we'd have had the mountain rescue teams out looking for us. It would have been a serious business, and it would have been no use saying that we knew where we were and what we were doing on that night trip down the mountain, because it would have been palpably untrue.

Notes

Introduction

1. Such a boat was kept by the Dukes of Norfolk on Ullswater, and Thomas Rose, in his 'descriptions' to Thomas Allom's celebrated drawings, says: "The firing of a cannon causes an awful uproar, as if the foundations of every rock on the lake were giving way." He also states that "a few wind instruments produce an entirely different effect: the most ravishing sounds fill the air, and form a thousand symphonies playing together from every part" . . . which suggests that there might also have been a resident orchestra.

Chapter 1

1. It is sometimes assumed that the name 'Sprinkling' derives from the area's fairly persistent rainfall, but its older name 'Sparkling Tarn' contradicts this assumption. It is said that the name really derives, in the tortuous way that such things happen, from the name of a Norse-period criminal, 'Prenti' (or 'branded') Bjorn, who found a refuge there and gave the tarn the name 'Prenti-Bjorns-tern'. The translation of that into 'Sparkling' or 'Sprinkling' Tarn is an unconfirmable exercise in etymology.
2. Records of the Coroner for the Honour and Lordship of Egremont.
3. 'Fluid' is meant to be read as 'flood'.
4. On dull holiday mornings, Cumbrians – and, no doubt, people in other parts of the country – still search the sky for "as much blue as will make a sailor a pair of breeches".
5. "Not the same."
6. See the author's *Lore of the Lake Country*.

Chapter 2

1. Hardwicke Drummon Rawnsley, honorary Canon of Carlisle Cathedral, second only to Wordsworth (in the opinion of the author) in importance among 'lakers' if only for the fact that he was a founder of the National Trust. He was also a prolific writer of poetry, and produced several well-researched books about the Lake District. He played a major role in the administration of local government, with emphasis on education and public health, and led the struggle to maintain the rights of way for the public in the Lake Country. An avid reader, he prepared himself for discussion on any projected topic. For example, in 1888 he attended a lecture at Keswick on the then new agricultural process of silage-making. Seen to be somewhat 'put about' when the meeting was breaking up, he explained that he had come prepared to deliver his own lecture on silage-making, and hadn't had the opportunity. The people of Keswick, ever-accomodating where the Canon was concerned, made amends and asked Canon Rawnsley to give his lecture on Silage the following week!
2. The 'Half-way House' on Skiddaw was a small hut, easily discernible because it was whitewashed regularly. Prices for refreshment there were high enough to cause complaint, but the keeper of the house needed reward for hauling supplies to such an altitude.
3. The 'senhora' was Southey's wife.
4. Southey's *Life* by Dowden.
5. Sir George Beaumont, patron of the Lake poets, who gave Wordsworth the small estate at Applethwaite which is the subject of Chapter 16.

Chapter 3

1. John I'Anson, after many successful years at the Royal Oak, retired to a house which he called 'The Acorns', because, as he put it, "it was the fruit of the Oak".
2. A sample of the old road in Borrowdale still exists. It is the road leading up to and past the Bowder Stone.
3. There were official guides for travellers who used the route over the sands, but some coachmen preferred to go it alone and pocket the guides' fees themselves.
4. Rough How Bridge, or 'Ruffa' as it was called by the locals, is still standing (see illustration). It was replaced by a new bridge

and road in 1904 and these are now a lay-by on the A591.

5. That the coachmen were of some standing is shown in thc interest taken in their off-duty activities by the local Press. The *Cumberland Pacquet* of 22 August 1826 reported that Henry Bowe, coachman of 'The Good Intent' between Keswick and Cockermouth, had raised an excellent crop of onions!
6. Mr Lighthouse was very critical of Lodore, first because the 'Boots' of the hotel was stationed at the wicket gate leading to the falls to collect fees from visitors to the falls – and hinting that sixpence was the least anybody paid, and second, because Lodore was having one of its frequent off-days and failing to live up to the image presented by Robert Southey.
7. The 'drag' was an iron shoe, attached to a chain, which was slipped under the wheel of the vehicle and, immbolizing the wheel as it was dragged along, acted as an effective brake. From the friction of rough road surfaces it became very hot, and it was a regular prank of the coachmen to ask an unpopular passenger to pick it up at the bottom of a hill. The passenger usually did not have to be asked to put it down again!

Chapter 4

1. 'Bet' here means, 'beat', 'bested' or 'defeated'.
2. *West Cumberland Times.*

Chapter 5

1. The Anglers' Hotel was demolished when it was planned to raise the level of the lake in the interest of Whitehaven's water supply. Afterwards it was discovered that sufficient water could be extracted from Ennerdale without raising its level, but efforts to have the hotel replaced have been thwarted.
2. In efforts to 'naturalize' the commercial forest-planting, the Forestry Commission have planted a considerable number of wild (or bird) cherry trees which are very pretty for a short season when in blossom, but which in that setting look more artificial than the plantings of Japanese larch and Sitka spruce.
3. Char fishing used to be carried on on a commercial scale at several of the lakes, including Ullswater, Windermere, Crummock, Buttermere and Ennerdale, and potted char was sold and sent to all parts of the country as a Lakeland delicacy. Ullswater lost its entire char population, probably due to pollution of the spawning becks by lead-mining operations, but

at Windermere there is commercial char fishing (by rod and line), and the fish are sometimes seen on Kendal market. In the rest of the lakes, char fishing has lost most of its popularity, mostly because successful char fishing is almost a forgotten art. Char was 'potted' by cooking it in a mixture of fat and vinegar. This is a method which removes completely the delicate flavour of the fish, and seems to have been devised as a means of preserving the fish long enough to withstand the journey to London. A modern char specialist recommends that the fish should be fried gently in butter.

4. *West Cumberland Times*, 11 November 1883.

Chapter 6

1. This is not an exaggeration. Some poachers used the leister, a trident-like weapon with three barbed points which was thrown at the spawning salmon from the bridge. As Thomas Farrall, famed dialect writer, said: "Theer a gravel bank at Yuse Brig whoar hundreds o' sammen mud be seen aboot Martinmas, spawning on what they cawt t' ridds . . . a greet temptation till a wurkin' man." The wholesale method of catching them was literally to trawl them out of the redds with a 'shackle' net which sometimes collected so many fish that the poachers stood as much chance of being dragged into the river as the salmon did of being dragged out of it.
2. "Hingin' in t' bell reaps" was the dialect term for the time which elapsed between the calling of the banns and the actual marriage.

Chapter 7

1. J.J. Armistead claimed to be the inventor of the grille of glass rods on which the ova rested in the hatching trays. The system is still in use in fish hatcheries.
2. As the Solway Fisheries.
3. *West Cumberland Times*, 3 July 1875.

Chapter 8

1. The estates of James Radcliffe, last Earl of Derwentwater, were attainted to the Crown for his part in the 1715 Rebellion, and were handed over to the Royal Naval Hospital, Greenwich.

Chapter 9

1. The author has not attempted the feat recently, but it used to be possible to shake hands with a friend through a hole under the Bowder's knife-edge base. You were supposed to make a wish and it would come true, but my physics teacher lived to a ripe old age!
2. The defensive walls of Castle How are still in good condition. It was a small Celtic hill fort, probably occupied during and after the Roman occupation. Its summit was artificially levelled in modern times, so there has been no reason for a systematic archaeological excavation.

Chapter 10

1. Tatie pot is made of potatoes, mutton, onions, and sometimes carrots. It is baked in an oven with a black pudding on top. Purists eat it with pickled red cabbage; non-gourmet Cumbrians don't mind pickled onions with it.

   Barley bannocks were large barley loaves baked in an oven, or, in an emergency, in the frying pan.

   Rum butter was originally developed as a sweet to celebrate a birth, probably a hangover from an ancient fertility rite. It is made of soft brown sugar, butter, rum and nutmeg.

   Stannin' pie is the true, classic Lake Country delicacy which has now almost disappeared. In Wasdale, stannin' pie was known by its other name, 'sweet pie', because it was made in a pie dish, and not in the form of a 'raised' pie as in some other dales.

   The Wasdale sweet pie was described by a Braithwaite lad who went visiting friends in Wasdale. Coming off Sty Head Pass, famished, he sat down to supper: "Yan o' t' things at they fetched oot fer supper was a real ooald fashioned sweet pie, an' as ye've nivver seed yan Ah mun tell ye aw aboot it.

   "Te begin wid, it was beak'd ev a pudden dish t'size ev a smaw cattle trough an' covered ower wid an inch an' a quarter o' crust; nin o' yer flaky puffed-up crust 'at crunch when t' knife gah's through, bit yan o' t' solid swort, 'at cuts quiet an' soft, like a bit o' cheese.

   "Inside on't was a mister o' currans an' raisins, an' spice an' sugar, wid a lock o' meat an' liver an' fat, aw cutten intil hauf-inch bits. In t' ceuken', t' fat hed risen till t' top an' set intil a ceake a quarter uv an inch thick on t' underside o' t' crust, while t' currans an' t' raisens an' t' meat were aw doon on t' bottom o' t' dish. Between t' crust and t' mince theer was a greasy mister uv spice an' gravy an' syrup, wid an odd lump uv fat floaten here an' theer."

2. A geld ram lamb.
3. The name Whillimoor is taken from a district in the parish of Moresby, and was given to most of the cheese made in Cumberland. It was the poorest of cheeses, and it ripened to a hardness that rivalled leather. In his *Cumberland Farming Life in Olden Times*, William Dickinson wrote:

   Their cheese wad rowl down a fell side like a wheel,
   Mappen hack it to bits wid a pick.

4. 'Taties and point'. Potatoes were boiled and dipped in a dish of fat or butter which was kept in the centre of the table. The 'point' came from an old fable that one farm family was so poor that the servants were only permitted to point their potatoes at the fat on the table; therefore the term 'taties and point' came to be used to suggest the most meagre of meagre rations.
5. There are several 'brick yubbens' left; none in use. One is in a barn at Brotherilkeld, Eskdale.
6. Powsowdy was a beverage for festive occasions. It was a mixture of rum and ale, spiced, and warmed with pieces of toast in it, and it was taken, like soup, with a spoon.

Chapter 11

1. Barely traceable on St Herbert's Island today are the footings of a small building, probably the remains of a chantry chapel which stood there when it became a place of pilgrimage.
2. For years after he had left, the site of the Skiddaw Hermit's roost could be identified by the pile of bottles and rubbish he had collected there.
3. This example of 'poetry', claimed to have been written by the Dodd Man, 'came to light' during a late nineteenth-century controversy in the local Press as to whether he was as good an artist as he was made out to be.

Chapter 12

1. See Chapter 10. Anybody who has lived on oatmeal porridge will agree that its flavour is unexciting. The method of first roasting the meal was often used when it was the staple of the dalesman's diet.

Chapter 13

1. Some accounts give the Shelleys' income as £400 a year.
2. *Literary Associations of the Lake District* by H.D. Rawnsley. To his credit, certainly not always to his profit, Rawnsley found "good in everything".
3. Calvert was ever ready to extend a helping hand when it was most needed. In 1814, when the Napoleonic Wars had driven the price of corn to a level which threatened famine for the poorer classes, he used his influence to have the summit of Lattrigg Common enclosed, had a road built to the top for the passage of ploughs, etc., and had it sown with corn in the hope that it would provide cheap food for the people. This experiment in high-altitude agriculture (Lattrigg is 1200 feet high) failed because the corn would not ripen.
4. This passage in his letter illustrates Shelley's arrogance.
5. *Life of Shelley* by E. Dowden.
6. ibid.
7. *Shelley's Early Life* by J. McArthy.
8. At Workington there had been large-scale immigration of Irish workers, encouraged by the Squire of Workington Hall, John Christian Curwen (in whom Shelley would have found a kindred spirit on the Irish question). This led to the infamous 'Croppies' riots of 1814, a series of attacks on Irish Catholics which ended in Curwen calling in the Army, with a detachment of Dragoons billeted on the town for several months.

   On 26 February 1812, Shelley was at Tanyrallt, and claimed he was attacked by an assassin who fired three shots at him. His story was not believed.
9. Five years after leaving Keswick, Henry Crabbe Robinson met Shelley at William Godwin's house, still abusive about Southey. Godwin also had 'progressive' ideas about marriage, and his wife, Mary Wollstonecraft, was one of the early advocates of women's rights. Her daughter Mary became Shelley's second wife, and wrote *Frankenstein*.

Chapter 14

1. It has been suggested, without much supporting evidence, that some of these 'intelligent' foxes were those which were hand-reared as pets in the late 1960s and early 1970s. At that time fox cubs were 'in fashion', but rapidly went out of fashion as they grew to adulthood and developed adult fox habits and aroma.

Many were turned loose or escaped.
2. In the lore of every foot-pack, and of most of the dales churches, there are stories of passing hunts which emptied churches (see below).
3. Sheep-worrying today is mostly by undisciplined domestic pets, often working in packs of two or three.

Chapter 15

1. The diligence of 'private' hunters in pursuit of the fox is proverbial in Lakeland. There have been several incidents of men with terriers returning to kill foxes holed up in what huntsmen have regarded as 'impregnable' spots. Their work does not meet with official approval. In 1875 a fox escaped hunters by finding a safe borran near Stickle Tarn. For three weeks a party of Langdale men worked there, night and day, blasting the rock by day and keeping the exit hole blocked with stones at night. After the three weeks a wet night drove them down the valley, and when they returned next day the stones had been removed and the fox had gone. Questions were asked around the district in an effort to discover who had been so unsporting as to give the fox a fighting chance, but without result, and it was eventually concluded that "Some Gursmere chap mud ha' done it", it being a recognized fact that the people of Grasmere, diluted as the tribe was by the infusion of off-comers, were not quite as keen on killing foxes as their Langdale neighbours.

Chapter 16

1. See Chapter 2.
2. Innovators in matters of public hygiene found the going particularly difficult in Cumberland. They were, in fact, ostracized at meetings and through the local Press for suggesting such innovations as piped water supplies and waterborne sewerage. Dr Lietch was given a particularly rough time at Keswick where, apart from the usual and almost universal objection on grounds that it would put up the rates, the inhabitants were convinced that they were living in the healthiest place on earth – despite the fact that the water supply (the River Greta), the sewerage disposal midden (a useful source of income because the compost was sold to farmers), and a large number of piggeries were in close proximity to each other.

3. *West Cumberland Times*, 23 August 1890.
4. William Henry Smith (1808-72), one of the less spectacular lakers, was born at Hammersmith, and came to Bowness-on-Windermere in 1848. One of his friends was Professor John Wilson ('Christopher North'), of Elleray. He also made Leitch's acquaintance and they eventually became firm friends. It was at Lietch's suggestion that Smith came to live in Keswick in 1852. In lodgings at 3 Derwentwater Place, he managed, however, to live a serene and uneventful life in near seclusion. He was in his mid-fifties when he met Lucy Cumming, who wrote short stories and translated German works, and who also lodged at 3 Derwentwater Place. They married and moved to Tent Lodge, Coniston, but soon returned to the Keswick district and took up residence at Newton Place in Borrowdale. He wrote extensively for *Blackwood's Magazine*. He died at Brighton.

Chapter 17

1. See the author's *Lore of the Lake Country*.
2. *Folk Speech of Cumberland and Some Counties Adjacent* by A.C. Gibson.
3. 'Joe and the Geologist' belongs to the time Gibson spent as local doctor for a large area extending from Ullock, where he lived, to Buttermere. He later removed to the Coniston area.

Chapter 18

1. Most of the writer's contemporaries and companions achieved that goal; the author's climbing career was cut off in its prime by a developing interest in ornithology, and an insane, headlong rush to join the Royal Navy at the outbreak of the 1939-45 war. The final blow came in May 1941, when, attempting to evade capture by the Germans, he nearly broke his neck. As the only 'experienced' mountaineer in the party, better was expected of him than demonstrating that the quickest way down a precipice was to fall.
2. It is certain, however, that a large number of the super-climbs listed in modern F.R.C.C. guides would have remained unclimbed, unclimbable if the young generation had not overridden old prejudices, and the game would have been the poorer for it.
3. It was not even considered to be correct procedure to leave slings hanging on the large chockstone in the Flake Crack, partly because it would have been considered an 'artificial aid'

to the next party up; partly because of an over-developed antipathy to litter; partly, in our case, because a few extra slings always came in useful, and we were usually hard up, financially.

4. Applause from passing hikers was one of those risks which had to be taken when climbing on the more popular, accessible crags. Our leader once jeopardized a very promising future in rock climbing's marble halls by doing a headstand on top of Napes Needle, purely for the entertainment of the crowd watching from the Dress Circle.
5. In those days, climbers had the choice of 'rubbers', which meant gymn shoes or plimsolls, or 'boots', which were nailed with soft iron 'ring-clinkers' which overlapped the edge of the sole and were ideal for rough, soft rock, or with 'tricounis', which were steel-toothed and gave a better grip on worn or harder rock. The 'vibrum' sole of a rubber composition came in time to save the crags from excessive wear and tear.

Glossary of Cumbrian Words and Phrases used in this Book

Chapter 4

Bet: beat, got the better of.
Cowper: trader (Cowp: to swap).
Towp: tip, dump, deposit.

Chapter 10

Barn: bairn, child. Anybody over eighty would call anybody under sixty 'Barn'.
Lish: lively.
Body: a person, usually female. 'T' owd body' usually meant 'mother'.
Foor-elders: forefathers.
Merry neets: Social gatherings for dancing, drinking and playing cards, usually at Christmas.
Greavv'd: dug.
Harden sark: A shirt of home-spun, home-woven linen, unpopular when new because of its roughness. Masters allowed their men to 'break in' new harden sark for them, but they became soft only after frequent launderings and unstinted use of the 'beatling stone' by the beck, lake, or riverside on which the dirt was literally beaten out of the garment.
Woo': wool.
Powsowdy: A drink for festive occasions. A mixture of ale and rum was heated in the set-pot and small pieces of toasted bread were floated in it.
Clash: Spoil, over-indulge.
Lig: lie.

Chapter 17

Es queer es Dick's hatband: Peculiar, as relating to people. Who Dick was, nobody knows, but his hatband was queer enough for it

to go ten times round, "an than it wadn't tie".
Gripe: garden fork.
A-keen: akin, related.
Herry: harry.
Despart: painful.
Stang: sting.
Stoundit: hurt.
Scowr't: scurried.
Feckless: harmless.
Gars: makes, compels.
Jee: go, wane, diminish
Durdem: 'Do', party, celebration; more generally, 'hubbub'.
Messet: Susannah Blamire's dancing messet was probably a monkey.
Feul: fool.
Esh: ash.
Kebby-stick: walking stick.
Hocker't: hobbled, limped.
Lonnin': lane.
Gedderen'-spot: gathering (or meeting) place.
Bladder: blather.
Foorneun: forenoon.
Gaily: very.
Thrang: busy.
Whyte: quite.
Smo': small.
Ebben: right, straight.
Rayder: rather.
Lang-nwos't: long-nosed.
Breist: breast.
Eddle: earn.
Mistean: mistaken.
Lowpin': leaping, jumping.
Scrafflin': scrambling.
Capp't: puzzled.
Pang'd: full, stuffed.
Pwoak: poke, bag.
Darrack: task (literally, day-work).
Soavin': salving. Salving time was one of the busiest times of the year for the fell sheep farmer.
Skeal Hill: Scale Hill, Loweswater.

Neist: next, adjacent.
As'd: asked.
Kaim't: keen, anxious.
Maislin': fool.
Toytle: topple.
Gurned: smiled (sometimes 'grimaced').
Bried: bread.
Hofe-thick: half-thick (thick-head; yet another of the many ways of calling a man a fool in the dialect).
Beak'd: baked.
Vannar: very nearly.
Lock: a little.
Mister: mixture.

Index

H

I

J

K

L